Brahms

A Listener's Guide

John Bell Young

AMADEUS
PRESS

An Imprint of Hal Leonard Corporation
New York

Published in 2008 by Amadeus Press
An Imprint of Hal Leonard Corporation
7777 West Bluemound Road
Milwaukee, WI 53213

Trade Book Division Editorial Offices
19 West 21st Street, New York, NY 10010

Printed in the United States of America

Book design by Snow Creative Services

Library of Congress Cataloging-in-Publication Data is available upon request.

ISBN: 978-1-57467-171-1

www.amadeuspress.com

Brahms

Unlocking the Masters Series, No. 15

For Michael Vincent Connolly

With love and gratitude

Contents

Acknowledgments ix

Introduction xiii

Chapter 1. Johannes Brahms: An Overview 1

Chapter 2. The Four Symphonies 9

Chapter 3. The Piano Music 45

Chapter 4. Violin Concerto in D Major, Op. 77 93

Chapter 5. Piano Quintet in F Minor, Op. 34 105

Chapter 6. *Ein Deutsches Requiem (A German Requiem)*, Op. 45 115

Appendix: Intonatsiia, or the Art of Listening 131

Glossary 141

Selected Bibliography 149

CD Track Listing 151

Acknowledgments

Writing about music, or any work of art governed by abstraction, is no easy task. One is easily persuaded by force of habit and by long-held beliefs in the veracity of a point of view, as if objectivity were the only thing that mattered.

But as musicians worth their salt know only too well, there are no ivory towers: music is so complex and abundant as to invite any number of perspectives. And where those perspectives are informed and imaginative, they are worthy of contemplation.

Much the same can be said of any artistic endeavor, and writing is no exception. I am indebted, for their assistance and advice, to a number of friends and colleagues, several of whom were not even aware that what I learned from them would contribute to it so substantially, and several of whom did not live to see the completion of this project.

Above all there is my late mother, Dorothy Burgess Young, without whose support and unflinching belief in my abilities I could never have written this volume or even so much as played a single note of music. Whether it was eerie coincidence or something born of a grander scheme, Amadeus Press offered me the formidable challenge of writing a dozen books for its distinguished roster only thirty minutes after my mother's passing in July 2007 at age eighty-eight. And so it is in honor of her that I commit to this enormous and challenging project.

There are in addition a number of individuals to whom I am indebted for their support and advice, literary and otherwise, while writing this book. First and foremost, I thank my best friend and partner, Michael Vincent Connelly, to whom this book is dedicated and without whom I could not have completed this task, for his uncompromising friendship, patience, solidarity, tireless assistance, and unwavering faith in my abilities and perseverance. I also extend my thanks to Joseph Early and Sandra Rush, whose infinite patience, innumerable kindnesses, critical overview, and thoughtful consideration were not only proof of the deepest friendship, but equal to the best editorial advice; Reni Santoni and Tracy Newman, without whose assistance and counsel at a time when I most needed it I would surely never have been able to complete these works; Eric Le Van, a magnificent pianist and a leading Brahms authority, whose encyclopedic knowledge and critical suggestions have been absolutely invaluable; Roberto Poli, Ian Lindsey, and Jonathan Tsay, each an extraordinary pianist and consummate artist, whose recordings, along with those of Eric Le Van, are included on the accompanying CD of this book; Stephen Hough, a great pianist and a gifted writer who took time out of his incredibly busy international schedule to have a look at my manuscript; Fred Maroth of Music & Arts Records, who provided many of the exquisite historic recordings, including those of Wilhelm Furtwängler and Ginette Neveu, that accompany this book; Michael York and Hugh Downs, both experienced authors whose support has been unwavering; Mark and Camilla Tarmy, whose understanding and generosity of spirit know no bounds, and who have patiently put up with my sometimes impossible demands for convenience and quietude; Margarita Fyodorova, who taught me all about intonation and much more; Rick Bechard, whose eye and ear as a documentary filmmaker were invaluable, as he helped me to reconsider both style and narrative, which I can only hope will find in these volumes a writer who does them justice; Gordon and Emily Jones, Joseph Fichter, Julie Marden, and others in the extended Putney School family, for their encouragement, kindness, and help; and John Cerullo, the publisher of Amadeus Press, for his goodwill and extraordinary demonstration of courage, in that he invested his faith and corporate resources in this longtime columnist and critic but untested book author. And thanks also to my editor at Amadeus Press, Jessica Burr, who is the best, and my meticulous copy editor Angela Buckley.

Finally, to those who are no longer with us, I extend my gratitude in ways that I can only hope will be borne aloft on the wings of angels. From these individuals I learned much of what I know of music. Among them are Constance Keene, a great pianist who was also my teacher and mentor for nearly thirty years; Michel Block, likewise among the great pianists of the twentieth century, whose musical savoir faire and personal gentility were a continual source of knowledge and enrichment; James Landrum Fessenden, a brilliant philosopher and musician whose premature death was a blow to all who knew him and whose willingness to share his phenomenally authoritative knowledge of any number of disciplines, from aesthetics to epistemology and psychoanalysis, has proven invaluable; Norwood and Cornelia Hinkle, whose exemplary years teaching music at the Putney School were an inspiration; and Claudio Arrau, Ernst Levy, and Andrzej Wasowski, the celebrated pianists who, in my few brief encounters with them, taught me more about music making than most could have done in a lifetime.

John Bell Young
Putney, Vermont
February 2008

Introduction

In this and future volumes for Amadeus Press, it is my objective to survey great music from a personal perspective, just as anyone would. Whatever I can convey of my ideas about listening, though informed by analytical scrutiny and historical data, will not be enslaved by technical analysis. While academia continues to do its job in the classroom, pointing out the idiosyncratic formalities of this or that composition as it teaches students to more effectively recognize compositional strategies, I prefer to do what I can to bring music to life in a kind of dialectical dance. These slim volumes for Amadeus Press, then, are part musical analysis and part interpretation, but above all a personal appreciation. My work here is not intended to be, nor should it be, construed as a work of scholarship.

Nowhere will I presume that the reader will be following my musical observations, or the accompanying CD, with a score in hand. So often when we listen to music, things seem to fly off the page of the score, or from the hands of the performer, in ways that strike us as inexplicably new and exciting, as if we had just heard the piece for the first time. Perhaps that's just how it should be. In any case, in attempting to put myself in the shoes of listeners, both those who are familiar with this music and those who may not be, I will do my best to bring them into the dynamic fold of the music as it reveals itself. And while there are certainly advantages to examining the score, there is also much to be said for letting your ears do what they do best when you trust your instincts: listening!

Among other things, I hope to establish a rapport with readers who may not be familiar with the technical terminology of music. Though I presume the reader has a minimal knowledge of the vocabulary of music, or access to information that would explain such things as meter, rhythm, note values, bar lines, and the array of Italian-language tempo and dynamic markings, I will nevertheless attempt to demystify some of the larger issues pertaining to musical experience.

To this end I will evaluate, describe, and convey as much as possible about compositional process and interpretation. Additionally, in several of these books I have invited a few extraordinary and exceptionally articulate professional musicians to contribute their ideas and commentary, as a way to look inside the mind and soul of performers as they perform. What a musician has to think about and actually do physically in order to play and interpret a musical composition is extraordinary and no easy feat. Musicians rarely take the opportunity to describe either their ideas or process to the public, which might benefit in some way from such a dialogue. At the very least, in allowing musicians to open up and reveal something of their most coveted ideas, individual points of view, and even frustrations with the work to which they are so uniquely committed, average music lovers, no matter their status, may come away with an enriched appreciation.

Thus as we begin this survey of Brahms's music, let's have a look at a few basic technical concepts, albeit nothing too intimidating. Let's start with the notion of *tonality*. What does that really mean?

If you think of a work of tonal music—music that depends for its very existence on the organization of its parts into tonal regions, or keys, and their relationships—as a kind of solar system, with planets, asteroids, meteors, light, and space, you will also have to conclude that somewhere or other there lurks a sun, too. And just about everything in this musically configured solar system orbits around that sun.

What I am getting at here is that the home key is akin to the sun, and its purpose similar. The home (tonic) key is a kind of sonorous landscape that gives sanctuary to all the parts of a composition and welcomes them home when they drift away or go off on their own into other keys. This tonal center exerts its own kind of gravitational pull, too. Everything in its sphere of influence moves inexorably toward it, and we experience this movement as fulfilling. The moment we return to the home key we sense a certain satisfaction, as if things were meant to return there all along. In turn, the parts of the composition—its rhythmically organized notes and motives—are irradiated by the heat of this musical sun, which not only envelops its progeny in its ever-present rays, but assures them of its power and permanence.

If I may digress for a moment, I would like to propose changing the paradigm for the discussion and analysis of music. For those who may not be so comfortable with technical terminology, whether it be fundamental or arcane, have no fear: while I could certainly refer to the home key of any tonal composition as the "tonic," or to its closest relations as the "dominant, subdominant, and mediant" (the common terminology of harmonic analysis), I prefer, for the purposes of this book, to deal with less technical matters and instead raise more experiential questions: How is it possible for our ears to recognize a musical event as it happens in real time, and once we do, how do we determine its significance? Are some events more significant than others? And while it's all well and good to identify the various elements of a musical composition by name, what use is that kind of exercise for listeners who are unable to do so?

To appreciate and recognize significant compositional events as they occur, it may prove more productive to focus our attention on the rhythmic and melodic progression of the work at hand. In other words, what we ought to ask ourselves as listeners is not to which key this or that chord belongs, or how the imposition of a Schenker graph would illuminate both form and harmonic structure, but something even more essential: Where are things—by which I mean melodies and rhythms—going, where did they come from in the first place, and how did they get there? By what visceral or aural means can listeners untrained in the vocabulary and complexes of music find their way "home" and back?

Think of it this way: all of us know very well our own home. We know how it is laid out, where the furniture is, where we've made open space or indifferently created clutter. If we are particularly well organized, we may even know what lurks in the darkest recesses of every closet and behind the rakes and shovels in the garage. Even during a power failure, when everything is thrown into total darkness, we can find our way around, though the gentle illumination of a small candle, even in a familiar place, would be welcome and could prevent us from stumbling over the unforeseen.

If this sounds like the stuff of an Alfred Hitchcock thriller, it is indeed possible to make an analogy to the genre of the mystery novel. Just as Agatha Christie keeps us on our toes in anticipation of whodunit, providing clues alluded to by the heroes and villains of her texts, so does a composer proffer information, albeit in musical categories. These musical clues are called *motives,* which are the musical equivalent to literary characters.

We can easily recognize a motive, no matter how brief, by its rhythm, pitch organization, melody, or mood. The eminently familiar first four notes of Beethoven's Fifth Symphony, for example, form the driving motive of that work. Composers worth their salt are resourceful, never failing to organize the elements of their music clearly and intelligibly so as to allow us to follow their train of thought. They will provide signposts and goals, and as the work progresses, they will develop, vary, and elaborate their materials. Eventually the home key—our "sun"—will reappear on the compositional horizon and beckon us back to the familiar place where the journey began.

Savvy listeners will strive to cultivate their listening habits and inscribe themselves within the musical activity, as if they are themselves creating the music as it unfolds in time. To a certain extent listeners, as real-time participants who process the stream of sound, are doing just that. In art music, complexity—that is, the myriad parts, rhythms, harmonies, and, not least, the relationships that each of these has to the other—is something not to be feared, but to be embraced. Listeners who are untrained in analysis and find themselves unable to name this or that compositional form, harmony, or technical particle should not be intimidated. Not everyone is a professional musician, or can be, and woe be unto a society replete with professionals but wanting for amateurs. In the final analysis, having an encyclopedic knowledge of music in all its details is unnecessary and unimportant for the nonprofessional music lover, because when it gets right down to it, what really matters is listening with an open mind and an open heart.

To this end we can, each and every one of us, decipher musical form, whether in its smallest incarnation (the motive), which is nothing more than a fragment of a larger picture, or in the larger format of a fugue or a sonata. Repetition is vital to understanding the architecture of musical form. Thus it is not without purpose, both structural and pragmatic, that the laws of composition have traditionally demanded the repetition of whole sections. As we listen to music, doing our best to follow its myriad melodies, fascinating rhythms, and changing harmonies, patterns emerge. These patterns embed themselves in our perception and memory. It is to these patterns that our ears become accustomed. Through this process, with the composer's help, the destiny of each motive evolves before our eyes (or, should I say, our ears) and "catches fire on form," to cite the German philosopher and music critic Theodor W. Adorno. Finally, a motive takes its place within the larger formal context it informs, influences, and ultimately helps to create.

The current volume concerns the music of Brahms and includes a survey of his major orchestral, choral, and piano music. As the vocal literature—that is, his songs—is plentiful and complex, I have concluded that it would not be in the best interest of those great works to attempt even a superficial survey here. Likewise, they deserve a volume of their own. Also, it is not the purpose of this book to break down or add to the abundant biographical materials about Brahms. Rather, it is my aim to demystify, from my perspective as a musician, the most salient elements of his music. I hope, too, to illuminate something of the thought processes that inform interpretation.

In writing this book, it became apparent that the viewpoints of other musicians would be both relevant and useful. The accompanying CD includes performances by three magnificent young pianists, Eric Le Van, Roberto Poli, and Ian Lindsey. We will meet Messieurs Poli and Lindsey in another of my books in this series, on Liszt, where their performances are as vivid and exceptional as they are poetic. Now they turn their attention to the early and late piano music of Brahms.

Likewise, Eric Le Van, a distinguished pianist and widely recognized Brahms authority, stands out as one of the most compelling interpreters of Brahms I've ever heard. Here he contributes his provocative thoughts about the composer and the art of interpreting his music. What is it, I asked him, that sets Brahms apart, from an interpreter's unique perspective, from other composers? Indeed, the next time you find yourself listening to a pianist play Brahms's Intermezzi Op. 118, or the lengthy Piano Sonata in F Minor, you might reflect on the enlightening commentary, included in these pages, of this exceptional artist.

Music is an adventure. If I am successful in cultivating in readers a renewed curiosity about its many recesses and shadows, rivulets and canyons, all the better. Certainly I make no claims to be right or wrong. The most rigorous harmonic and formal analyses are probably better taken up by theorists and scholars, whose work is more useful to each other than to nonexpert music lovers. The latter, after all, are those who simply strive to become as intimate with musical experience as they can without becoming scientists. It is to those *amateurs de la musique* that I dedicate this volume and who I hope will find within its pages something of value.

Brahms

Johannes Brahms: An Overview

As the story goes, Johannes Brahms, bored at a glittering society event at one of Vienna's more prestigious palaces, couldn't contain himself. Feeling trapped amid an impressive gathering of luminaries and lingering literati, he sought escape from the small talk. After all, for the solitary and private Brahms, to engage in anything but substantive conversation, if he had to converse at all, was a waste of valuable time. Acutely aware, too, of his status as an international celebrity, he vigorously declined to be drawn into a world of superficial adulation and hangers-on. He was not comfortable in large crowds, nor in unfamiliar company, and preferred instead the companionship of longtime colleagues and old friends.

Fed up with the din of polite conversation, Brahms, his hefty girth oddly complemented by his long white beard, stood up, excused himself publicly, and said, "If there is anyone here I have failed to insult, please forgive me!"

True or not, that endearing tale is one that paints Brahms, the man as well as the composer, with a fair degree of accuracy. While he was not known to have a hot temper, it was no secret that he was a loner whose need for solitude was artistically inspired and pragmatic. He could be rude or dismissive when he had to be, but behavior of that sort was for him the exception, not the rule. He abhorred playing out his life or creative procedures in public, and the notion of using his position to make known his darkest critical views, as Richard Wagner so often did, was anathema to him. Nor did he have any particular interest in, or even liking for, the innumerable honors society sought to bestow on him; indeed, he lost no sleep at all when he twice turned down, in 1877 and again in 1892, an honorary doctorate from Cambridge University. (He did accept a similar honor, closer to home, from the University of Breslau in 1879.)

But Brahms was equally known for his unselfish willingness to help, encourage, and even finance other gifted composers. He was a tireless coach of the musicians in whom he saw potential, taking time out of his enormously busy professional life to advise and help them in any way he could. He was generous even to those who, like Wagner, loathed him and considered him a kind of public enemy by virtue of the kind of music he was writing. Brahms was a purist of sorts who rigorously declined, throughout his life, to assimilate anything that so much as smacked of program music. For him, drama, as well as the extramusical associations that were bound up with it, gained value only when it emanated from within the musical work, rather than being imposed, with superficial artifice, from without. The notion of virtuosity, too, as something either implicitly necessary or equal to the complexities of compositional process, struck him as ludicrous.

A scholar of early music, editing whole volumes of the music of Rameau and Couperin, with a special interest in the choral music of the Renaissance and baroque eras, Brahms was a throwback in some ways to the traditions and sensibilities of an earlier time. Rejecting the demands of his own era, which would have preferred to see any gifted young composer also assume the rigorous schedule of a performing virtuoso, Brahms settled rather comfortably into a different sort of life. And while, like any committed composer, he was only too happy to perform his own music, he turned away from anything resembling a concert career; neither the music nor the life of his contemporary Franz Liszt appealed to him in the least. Intuitive of his destiny, and assured of his future, he set about his life patiently, with the pragmatic diligence of one who takes no chances. Brahms constructed his career as much as he fell into it; whatever luck might have come his way, whatever useful and determinative influences fueled his ambitions, and whatever private or public favor or even disinterest he might have curried were all things and events that he deliberated and cultivated with aforethought.

To say that Brahms was a man who didn't bruise easily might be unfair, as he was, after all, human. And yet, in spite of the insults and disparagements that others, particularly Richard Wagner, saw fit to throw his way, he remained, in a word, imperturbable. He was neither vindictive nor confrontational, preferring to react to such criticism in quite another way: through his music. And as we shall see, he did so by means of codification or, more specifically, allusion.

Born in Hamburg on May 7, 1833, into a musical family, Brahms was enamored of symphonic music from an early age. His father was a double bassist in the Hamburg Philharmonic. Though his lack of a formal education was a sore point throughout his life, Brahms always enjoyed a healthy curiosity about all things intellectual. He was seven years old when he took his first piano lessons with one Otto F. W. Cossel; in Russian musical circles, that would be considered a late start destined to compromise precocity. Isolated from the mainstream, the young Brahms had little knowledge of the music of Chopin or Liszt; ironically, that he did not worked to his advantage. Indeed, it was his naiveté that allowed him to indulge wholly original musical fantasies of his own invention, thus distinguishing his compositional vocabulary and style from other composers'.

In 1846, at Cossel's prodding, Brahms, who had already expressed more interest in composition than in performing, went to Eduard Marxsen (1806–1887), a prominent Hamburg pianist and composer. It was on Marxsen's recommendation that he made his first attempt to contact Robert Schumann, but the effort failed when the sample of his work he hoped Schumann would at least examine was returned to him unopened. Nevertheless, under Marxsen's tuition, music, art, and literature became for him an extended family on which he could rely for sustenance; these became the measure of his humanistic *Weltanschauung* and of his own faith, which he interpreted in an entirely individual manner, as his magnificent *German Requiem* would later demonstrate so profoundly. He was a spiritual man—but not a zealot—who happened to value the wisdom of the Bible he came to know so well. But he also refused to blindly subscribe to the ersatz representations that human beings, in the guise of acolytes, made in the name of a personified God.

By all accounts Brahms was a fine pianist, a proficient horn player, and a passable cellist, though not one given to playing all the right notes all the time. His objectives were to make music and to use his abilities as both a performer and a composer to serve art, but not to serve himself in the creation of it. This attitude earned the respect of both Robert and Clara Schumann, to whom he was introduced by his friend the violinist Joseph Joachim. He met the Schumanns at their home on September 30, 1853, and with that, his fate was sealed. He respected and adored them both and found in them like-minded spirits. After Robert's death in 1854, he turned to Clara, at first in the naive but youthful hope that this older woman and distinguished concert pianist would return his romantic infatuation in ways that went beyond friendship. As far as anyone knows, and in the absence of any concrete evidence to the contrary, their relationship indeed blossomed, but only into the platonic sphere of close confidence and collegial endearment.

Brahms reviled mediocrity. He routinely destroyed his own works, dissatisfied with anything that might survive, thanks to popular interest, without deserving it on aesthetic and artistic grounds. He had no desire whatsoever to have his name associated with any work of art that could not be objectively evaluated, in musical as well as historical categories, as both revelatory and enduring. Thus what for some might have seemed merely fetishistic was for him a matter of artistic necessity. His temperament, fueled by solitude and self-awareness, favored an almost monolithic patience. To this end, he was careful to harvest and set aside the best of his ideas even at times when he had no particular place to house them compositionally.

That he so frequently reinvented his music, recasting it in new forms until he got it just right, was itself a consequence of his steely self-discipline and Brahmin-like willingness to appease the gods of patience. For Brahms, the creation of a musical composition was never a matter of professional adjudication, or even determination, but an organic process that demanded forethought, reflection, and above all maturity. And those things in turn required time or, more specifically, the *passage* of time. Just as time and gestation imbue a great wine with its bouquet, harmonic resonance, and ambrosial fragrance, so does time condition, enrich, and enliven art, imbuing it not merely with the spirit and thoughts of its creator, but with an autonomous existence that allows it to mature, endure, and thrive for generations to come.

Acutely aware of what his work might mean for posterity, and thus for civilization, Brahms astutely but firmly rejected any activity—be it a public interview, an academic honor, or even the composition of music the sole purpose of which was to make money—that might later be construed as selfish and superficial. Given the abundant fruits of his labors, and what he in fact left behind, we can easily see now, in retrospect, why he did so.

For a long while, and well into his thirties, Brahms, who had already settled in Vienna with the enthusiastic endorsement of the Schumanns, had found a certain satisfaction as a choirmaster. Though at one time he had his heart set on becoming the director of the Hamburg Philharmonic, he abandoned that idea when the august institution snubbed him in favor of a singer, Julius Stockhausen. With that, he resigned himself to accepting an appointment, with only the slimmest support, as the leader of the Vienna Singakademie. He led this ensemble in a cappella music of Renaissance and baroque composers, including Heinrich Schütz and J. S. Bach. It would be five more years before he took up permanent residence in Vienna, but no matter; in the interim he lavished most of his time and attention on composing, bringing forth such works as the F Minor Piano Quintet, the D Minor Piano Concerto, the G Major String Sextet, the E Minor Cello Sonata, the Paganini Variations for piano, more than a dozen songs, and, last but not least, the *German Requiem*.

With the death of his mother in 1865, Brahms was inspired to compose and finally bring to completion the *Requiem* he had so long had in mind. Its creation was a seminal event that changed his life forever. It took only three performances of the work, in various stages of incompletion, to persuade the public, and indeed the world, that in Johannes Brahms was a very great composer indeed, one equal to Beethoven and Bach. In 1869, Brahms found himself a subject of public adulation; he had become, in a word, a star. And with that status came all manner of accolades, invitations, commissions, influence, and wealth beyond anything he had ever known, much less expected.

That this sort of recognition in his lifetime was possible was evidence enough of how far music, by that time widely accepted as an art worthy of serious contemplation, had come with regard to its social and even professional status. While his success riled some, including the self-serving Wagner, who had fully expected to inherit Beethoven's throne and rule the musical world unchallenged, it served only to embarrass Brahms, who made every effort to see it for what it was—ephemeral, vain, and wholly inconsequential to his compositional aesthetics.

Brahms never married, having seen in that institution an implicit responsibility that he dared not assume. He was fully aware of the price a commitment to wife and family would extract from him, and, equally cognizant of his universal gifts and destiny, he resolved to avoid such ties. He refused to put himself in a position that would compromise his life work or hurt, however unintentionally, anyone who got in the way of it. And so he remained a bachelor all his life, his relationships with women rarely blossoming into more than a series of dates and, in the best instances, warm and lasting friendships.

As for his compositional style, well, a great deal has been said and written. It is not my intention nor within the scope of this book to move into that subject with the rigorous analytical zest that so many scholars, including Geiringer, Swafford, Schauffler, Stuckenschmidt, Schoenberg, Notley, and Beller-McKenna, have invested. Suffice it to say that, as a young man, Brahms found himself enamored of Hungarian music, as were so many others in the late 1840s. That is because in 1848, the Austrians, then all-powerful, and the Russians, aspiring to the same, put down a near-revolution in Hungary. Driven by their enemies from their home territory, hundreds if not thousands of Hungarian freedom fighters—what today we call insurgents—jawboned their way through Europe, bringing with them the colorful customs, fashion, art, and music of their homeland. Even Liszt, who left Hungary as a child, couldn't claim this authenticity for himself and thus, like other composers, could give voice to the indigenous fantasies of his childhood only by composing his own brand of Hungarian music.

Brahms, an echt-German provincial of Lutheran stock, found this music exotic and aspired to find a way to incorporate it imaginatively into his own compositions. He studied its litany of bizarre, angular, and often irregular cross-rhythms, gave voice to its intoxicating streams of triplets and to the so-called Gypsy scale (C, D, E-flat, G, A-flat, B, C$'$), and came to admire the frenetic *czárdás,* with its propulsive duple meter. Despite the dubious authenticity of such music—often it was more style than substance, created and played ad hoc by street musicians—there were at least some authentic elements. One can only speculate what conclusions Brahms would have come to, or how his music might have been influenced by the findings and experiments of Béla Bartók and Zoltán Kodály, who scoured their native land in search of Hungary's indigenous folk music.

Brahms, perhaps as a means of holding on to his values and keeping to himself, was fond of composing in the countryside and produced his best works while on holiday. In 1890, he tried in vain to announce his retirement, but he couldn't resist the call of the muse. In his last years he composed, in addition to a number of brief but highly complex piano works, the A Minor Clarinet Trio, the B Minor Clarinet Quintet, and two clarinet sonatas. Evidently something of the melancholy sound of that instrument appealed to him in his waning years, as if it were an emblem of his mortality.

When Clara Schumann, the one person he loved more than anyone save his mother, died in May 1896, something of Brahms died, as well. Less than a year later, on April 2, 1897, Brahms, too, gave up the ghost. He was accorded military honors and laid to rest in Vienna's central cemetery next to Beethoven and Schubert.

The Four Symphonies

Though Brahms penned only four symphonies, his reputation as perhaps the greatest symphonist after Beethoven had already been established during his lifetime. Even so, the remarks of some of his staunchest advocates were known to jar him. Indeed, his friend Eduard Hanslick, a preeminent critic, embarrassed Brahms when he declared the Third Symphony to be the new "Eroica." The composer cringed just as much when the Second Symphony was likened, with dreary disregard, to Beethoven's "Pastoral."

Always the perfectionist, Brahms was not comfortable with anything he composed unless it met his rigorous standards. The number of sketches, incomplete pieces, and even completed manuscripts he threw on the logs could likely have filled the Library of Congress. Brahms was as merciless a critic of his own work as he could be of others'. His self-criticism led him to work at a pace, often slow, that befitted his temperament and maximized his creative juices. It sometimes took him years to complete a single work, or to recast it in another form more suitable to the material, or, alternatively, to restore a work already thus transformed to its original state. This tendency to rework his material was not due to any lack of confidence on his part but was rather a measure of his resourcefulness. It could even be construed as a particularly ingenious career strategy that allowed his abundant ideas time to mature.

There was, and perhaps still is, a long-held superstition among composers that anyone who lived to write nine symphonies, as Beethoven did, would not live to write another. After Beethoven's death in 1827, composers ran scared, preferring to consolidate their symphonic output

into just a few major works. With that, the quest for the musically monumental had begun, though only a few would satisfy it with anything
substantial. Berlioz and Schumann each penned massive symphonies,
and on the cusp of the twentieth century, Mahler and Bruckner did
the same.

Other great composers, such as Chopin, did not even touch the
genre. Evidently, intimidated by superstition, no one wanted to risk
dying young or in advance of fulfilling his creative potential. Indeed,
Mahler did not survive to compose his Tenth Symphony (sketches of
which were later fleshed out by others), though *Das Lied von der Erde*
would certainly qualify as a symphonic work.

As we have seen, Brahms often expressed his distaste with being
compared to Beethoven, whom he idolized. But it is unlikely that anything as commonplace as superstition influenced his decision to write
only four symphonies. On the contrary, the number of works that he
could have composed in any genre was unimportant—their ultimate
aesthetic worth was what mattered. Brahms's symphonies, which
enjoyed enormous critical and popular success in his lifetime, stand out
as models of compositional integrity. While his protagonists have long
held them to be the antithesis of romantic excess in light of the classicism that informs their construction, they are nonetheless creatures of
romanticism: lush, opulent, ardent, and intensely expressive.

Even so, the essentially romantic ethos that informs them in no
way compromises their complexity. While detailed analyses in compositional, aesthetic, and even semiological categories are beyond the
scope of this slim volume—to do critical justice to even one of Brahms's
symphonies would require a book at least twice the length of this one—
there is one salient element common to them all that merits discussion,
and that is *allusion.*

In one of the more provocative papers on Brahms's music, "Allusive
Irony in Brahms's Fourth Symphony," Kenneth Hull draws attention
to the role of allusion in the composer's symphonic music, though he
hardly stops there:

> Allusion is understood to be a purposeful, extracompositional
> reference made by means of a resemblance, usually thematic and

local in nature. It is a stylistic device employed by a composer to direct the attention of the listener to the passage that is alluded to, and to the larger context in which it appears. When the full potential of allusion is exploited, an allusion will suggest secondary resemblances or resonances that relate the two works in further meaningful ways. . . . Allusion is not really a species of borrowing, although the presence of resemblance, or even exact quotation, may superficially suggest as much. In borrowing, identification of the source material is irrelevant to our aesthetic appreciation of the work and is usually not desired by the composer. . . . In allusion, on the other hand, recognition of the resemblance is essential, and our attention is directed away from the later work toward the earlier one.

Thus numerous allusions that pepper Brahms's symphonies and other works, according to Hull, are neither coincidental nor verbatim citations. Instead, their occurrence, and moreover, their *manner* of occurrence, is no less significant than their thematic, rhythmic, or instrumental resemblance. In positioning allusive references to the music of other composers, Brahms (who was certainly not the first nor the last to do so) engages in a kind of critical commentary that is as musically informed as it is socially relevant and, in some instances, wholly personal. The exemplification of another composer's thematic schema is no mere exercise. On the contrary, the cultivation of musical allusion brings along with it not only a batch of notes and rhythms, but also something of the context that informed its source.

An allusion might not be innocent, either; more often than not, it provided Brahms (as it certainly did Schumann and Beethoven before him) an occasion to alter or even invert the meaning, compositional or metaphorical, of another's work. For example, where the Andante of Beethoven's Fifth so confidently sings out its second principal theme, which plays a recurring role throughout that mighty work, the mood it sets is one of victory, and of *overcoming* adversity—the sine qua non of late classical-era aesthetics. And yet Brahms, in the Andante moderato of his own Fourth Symphony, reinvents that figure as something tragic, making of it a final denouement that runs out of energy and resigns itself, unlike Beethoven's, to the minor key that spawned it.

Not everyone within earshot will grasp a composer's allusion, be it literary, textual (as they are so abundantly in the *Requiem*), or strictly compositional (i.e., where allusion is limited to notes and rhythms absent any implied or accompanying text, such as a libretto or a liturgical setting). Compositional allusion, in particular, engages in a kind of abstraction that, while aesthetically significant, may escape the average listener. Even so, music lovers, no matter their background, can think of such occurrences as a species of classical irony, provided they have occasion to learn something about them ahead of time. Citing (but not alluding to!) Mark Evan Bonds, Kenneth Hull offers a succinct definition:

> "In rhetoric, irony is a trope by which the speaker, through various clues like gesture, tone of voice, or context, conveys precisely the opposite of what he says (e.g., 'For Brutus is an honorable man')." The distinction between the attitude of a speaker and the content of his utterance is not one that lends itself readily to instrumental music. . . . Yet the referential character of allusion does allow this distinction to be approximated in music. In the case at hand, the resemblance in pitch and rhythm that permits Brahms's allusion[s] to be recognized constitutes the denotative "content" of the allusion; but by altering the dynamic level, instrumentation, and harmony, Brahms creates a differing mood or "attitude."

The conveyance of such "ironic" elements becomes, in significant ways, an obligation of the performer. Allusion, if thoroughly surveyed, can indeed play a definitive and altogether pragmatic role in musical interpretation. A savvy conductor, for example, aware of such moments, may strive to draw attention to them in subtle ways, be it rhythmically, through the discreet acceleration or slackening of tempo; through slight prolongations of specific harmonies or pitches; or through dynamic modulations that may not always conform to the composer's specific, written instructions.

Eric Le Van, the pianist and leading Brahms interpreter whose recordings are featured on the CD that accompanies this book, finds more than a little mystery in Brahms's use of allusion. In his paper "Brahms and the Fabric of Memory," Le Van digs deep:

Brahms seemed to have sensed to the core of his being this poetic power of allusion. Because of such awareness, and notwithstanding his rejection of the most outwardly innovative forms of his time, he appears strikingly modern. Not until the advent of modernist literary models do we find such habile weaving of allusion into the very fabric of complex structures; allusion not only to exterior sources, but within and between the various movements of the same work. In the latter case—most pronounced in the F minor sonata—he creates a world within itself, a hermetic prism whence the stuff of memory derives and is refracted throughout. . . . By no means did Brahms limit his range of references to the prime matter of his musical predecessors. An inhabitual hybrid of other musical—as well as extra-musical—sources was to constitute his private, sui generis reservoir, a reservoir from which he was to dip periodically for the remainder of his life. Included are folk song, the Nordic ballad, the light fare comprised of popular ditties, dance tunes, potpourris . . . the fantastical world of E. T. A. Hoffmann; the dream-like landscapes of Tieck and Jean-Paul; the poetic atmosphere of Scottish moors and legends. *He knew too well that for a musical passage to evoke the mystery of a distant voice from the past, it must somehow echo another passage formerly heard and stored in one's memory—the artist's and the listener's.* (emphasis added)

Certainly Brahms disavowed any connection to or even interest in composing program music. Though he wrote nearly two hundred songs, he never composed an opera. His music, no matter how self-referential in strictly compositional categories, codifies intimacy and passion in a way that few, save Bruckner and Mahler, would be able to duplicate. And neither Bruckner nor Mahler, in spite of the grandeur of their symphonic works, ever garnered in their lifetimes quite the international public adulation that Brahms did. That is not to suggest that the symphonies of Brahms are in any way superior to theirs. But something about his individual compositional language—a musical vocabulary that codifies warmth, inwardness, sincerity, consolation, and earnestness—continues even now to move our sensibilities and affections.

Symphony No. I in C Minor, Op. 68

2 Flutes, 2 Oboes, 2 Clarinets, 2 Bassoons, Contrabassoon,
    4 Horns, 2 Trumpets, 3 Trombones, Timpani, Violins 1 and 2,
    Violas, Cellos, Basses
Initial sketches drafted in 1856; composition begun in earnest in
    1862 and continued over a period of fourteen years
Premiere at Karlsruhe on November 4, 1876, Hans von Bülow,
    conducting

First movement: Un poco sostenuto; Allegro
Second movement: Andante sostenuto
Third movement: Un poco allegretto e grazioso
Fourth movement: Adagio; Più andante; Allegro non troppo,
    ma con brio

Given the lengthy gestation period of this symphony—nearly fifteen years elapsed between the composer's initial sketches in 1852 and its first performance in 1876—it is perhaps no wonder that its titanic character has led more than one critic to refer to Brahms as the rightful heir to Beethoven. Indeed, at the work's premiere in 1876, the preeminent conductor and pianist Hans von Bülow, mesmerized by its power and ardency, proclaimed it as the "tenth"—a none-too-subtle reference, of course, to the symphony that Beethoven might have written had he lived. The compliment was great, but it embarrassed the solitary and taciturn Brahms, a loner whose curious doubt in his own abilities as a symphonist was already well-known by that time.

Though his first outing in symphonic form, this is in many ways Brahms's most significant symphony. Perfectionist or not, that it took him nearly twenty years to complete it is less a testimony to any lack of confidence on his part than it is to his egoistic aspiration to total authority, to speak nothing of his long-term ambitions. He was not about to let the other side of the famous romantic debate on aesthetics get the better of him, nor to allow the disparagement of Wagner and his coterie of dramatists to compromise his sensibility.

Brahms was forty-three years old and already a celebrated composer in Europe when the First Symphony made its debut. His reputation as a perfectionist preceded him. He destroyed the slow movement after the premiere of an early version of the work in 1867. Virtually nothing survives of his sketches for a first symphony in D minor, which he penned in 1854. A two-piano arrangement of that work was never published. Nevertheless, Brahms didn't abandon his ideas completely, harvesting three of its four movements for inclusion in subsequent compositions. To that end, its scherzo found a place in his *German Requiem,* while the First Piano Concerto (also in D minor) became the beneficiary of material from the first and second movements.

First movement: Un poco sostenuto; Allegro

No one is likely to argue that the steady, uninterrupted beat of the timpani, which press forward in 6/8 time with merciless tenacity for the first eight bars of this movement, fails to define the edgy, turbulent mood. Indeed, in the scant thirty-seven bars that constitute the introduction, Brahms introduces no fewer than three fragmentary motives, which he will eventually combine to form a single, unified melody.

The first of these motives, which proves vital to the work's overall formal construction and emotional power, is a terse, intense chromatic ascent. It is entrusted to the violins and cellos, and it pleads its case beneath a rich procession of thirds in the winds astride an eight-bar-long pedal point on C. This brief though expressive theme is nothing if not an evocation of pain, more so than longing, as if its very survival depends on the mood it hoped to establish. Denying any sanctuary to strong beats, at the beginning of and middle of the bar lines, Brahms avails himself of hemiola to engender tension in this theme. You can think of hemiola, a central part of Brahms's musical vocabulary, as a kind of substitute; as the *Harvard Dictionary of Music* aptly describes it, *hemiola* refers to "the use of three notes of equal value in the time normally occupied by two notes of equal value."

Indeed, the *fortissimo* reiteration of the same theme only nineteen bars into the work may at first deceive the listener into believing that things could not possibly become any more intense. But they do. Though it may appear, even at this early stage, as if the movement has reached a premature climax, something more substantial is at work. Here, the two additional, entirely distinct, motivic fragments are introduced, lending the symphonic fabric its character. On the heels of the ardent first theme, some nine bars into the work, a litany of sixths, quiet, distended, and likewise modified in hemiola and accompanied by the strings plucking in pizzicato, are entrusted to the woodwinds and, in contrast, provide relief from the foregoing urgency. Only a few bars later, the strings, offering yet another motivic strand—in the form of an E-flat major arpeggio—swell from a dulcet *pianissimo* to the most brazen *fortissimo*. An unaccompanied oboe connects the introduction to the main body of the exposition with a plaintive wail repeated by the cellos. It is not so much a climax that is reached in the twenty-third bar as it is the culmination of the motivic materials up to this point.

With the arrival of the *exposition* (which in sonata form is responsible for introducing all the principal themes in advance of their elaboration in the *development* and their varied return in the *recapitulation*), Brahms has, in effect, already rendered familiar to his listener all the major motivic materials. But he has plenty of surprises left up his sleeve. With the pugnacious thrust of the timpani and woodwinds giving staccato voice to a lone eighth-note, the exposition is inaugurated. Without delay, the three motives, now juxtaposed, resume their symphonic status as advocates for a complex counterpoint, again assigned to the strings. The arpeggiated motive takes momentary precedence before being set aside and on top of the motive in sixths, with the suggestion of the opening chromatic figure never very far away.

The arpeggio motive, unable to resist drawing attention to itself, resumes its prominence for a short while en route to a new, somewhat ethereal variant of the opening chromatic figure. Here, the oboe is quietly thrust into the symphonic spotlight against the cellos, which complement it with a pulsating echo of the arpeggio motive. The oboe, refusing to give up its lead, emerges with an ostensibly new motive only a few bars later. This figure, which combines characteristics of both the arpeggio and sixths motives, is something on the order of a sigh; it weeps the collective consciousness of its motivic brethren. Then, in a moment reminiscent of the first movement of Beethoven's Fifth, the strings alight in punctuation on three eighth-notes, played pizzicato before enlarging to a *fortissimo* and set astride the arpeggio motive, now turned on its head in inversion by the bassoons and cellos. The exposition's blustery codetta is enriched further when this three-note figure, still under the command of the strings and bassoons, is offered in counterpoint to the first principal motive, whose ardency has hardly abated. What's more, an unusual modulation to E-flat minor on the cusp of the ensuing development contributes to the underlying tension, even uneasiness, of this cadential denouement.

The development section, as befits its stature in the canon of classical music, wastes no time in making claim to the materials it has been charged with elaborating. The copious flats that had transformed C minor to E-flat minor only moments earlier, at the close of the exposition, are now enharmonically transformed into sharps, leading the work into yet another remote and unexpected key, B major. The heretofore quiescent arpeggio motive is now newly outfitted in a most strident *fortissimo* and, though again assigned to the strings, is copiously covered by the woodwinds in thirds. What's more, it is cast now not as accompaniment, counterpoint, or simple presentation, but in the form of a canon between the violins and the cellos. As a canon—which the *Harvard Dictionary of Music* succinctly describes as "the imitation of a complete subject by one or more voices at fixed intervals of pitch and time"—its confidences are now revealed in a kind of dialogue among the instruments. But just as this has gotten under way, the violins dimly echo, in the guise of a descending melody, the ethereal motive introduced by the oboes toward the end of the exposition. This "new" thematic construction may also be related to a transitional passage in the exposition, in which the violins, playing in a jaunty unison of pizzicatos, usher in the codetta. Brahms is relentless in his treatment of the motive in sixths and the arpeggio motive, which flesh out the rest of the development. In anticipation of the recapitulation, a long pedal point on the dominant pitch of G drones forcefully in the bass and bassoon, adumbrated by the dark rumbling of the timpani astride them. A modulation to a most remote and unexpected key—B minor—might at first appear to throw off the trajectory of the movement, but Brahms's compositional strategy here suggests something rather different: the change of key becomes a means to heighten ambiguity and thus create even greater tension at the movement's eleventh hour.

The recapitulation, foreshadowed by the woodwinds and strings, now in unison as they travel in chromatic descent, augurs a return to the tonic C minor. Certainly this return to the home key belies any overt rejection on Brahms's part, no matter the principled innovations of harmony and rhythm this symphony has to offer, of compositional convention. Indeed, the recapitulation repeats almost verbatim the materials of the exposition, with relatively little variation and much in conformity with standard sonata form, where just about everything bears repetition in the tonic, rather than migrating to the dominant.

The coda is a brusque and nervous affair, availing itself of steeply descending intervals of minor thirds, first introduced toward the end of the exposition, as a way to conclude the movement's business. Played at once *fortissimo* and pizzicato, this figure is intermittently punctuated by major thirds in the woodwinds and a steady reiteration of B-flats by the horns and trumpets. The chromatic motive of the opening, reassigned to the woodwinds, brings the work to a close, though now in the presence of the timpani and horns, which regurgitate the pedal point of the introduction. The concluding chord, a C major triad, is perhaps a testimony to the composer's audacity, in that it confronts the austere pessimism of the prevailing tonality.

Second movement: Andante sostenuto

The opening bars of this no-less-expressive rondo movement look back to the introduction of the first movement and in doing so embrace a whisper of its sister movement's opening motive. It moves, too, from the metrical organization of the Allegro in 6/8 time to a stately 3/4. Indeed, if the first and last movements of this symphony pay homage to Beethoven's Fifth and Ninth symphonies, then the first measures of this lovely Andante sostenuto evoke the variation movement of Beethoven's Piano Sonata Op. 109, likewise in E major.

The string-rich presentation of the principal theme, accompanied by the thinnest halo of bassoons and horns, is a consolation of sorts that embraces the listener with such warmth, dignity, and melancholy as to suggest Brahms's agenda was more personal than universal, as if he were speaking to a single person. Perhaps in writing it he had his mother in mind; she died in 1867 just as he was working in earnest on this symphony.

Some seventeen bars into the movement, a lone oboe emerges with tentative assurance as it gives voice to a theme of immeasurable tenderness and longing. This is followed by yet a new theme, taken up by the first violins and accompanied by gentle rocking, in dotted notes, from the violas and bass below. It comprises a chromatic melodic strand that angles upward in syncopes before falling back to the alto register in a stream of sixteenth-notes. The oboes, followed by the clarinets, then return with a dulcet subordinate theme, also in sixteenths, that bears some relation, at least in its rhythmic design, to the theme that preceded it. The strings then take over, accompanied by a gentle river of descending double thirds in the winds.

The principal theme returns, now enriched by the darker hue of the violas, and precedes the reprise of the theme of longing carried by a solo oboe in the first pages of the movement. Most remarkable is the transition from the foregoing development to this recapitulation; the mood is mysterious, vague, making capital of its ethereal harmonic ambiguity as the timpani purr in *pianissimo* just beneath the surface. But now a solo violin, accompanied by a French horn and an oboe in the musical distance, assumes its lyrical responsibility as it serenely elaborates the serpentine melisma in a quiescent coda.

Third movement: Un poco allegretto e grazioso

The rustic character of this movement is buttressed by the simplicity of its presentation. The key has again changed, as Brahms paints his ideas in A-flat major, the favored key for bucolic indulgence. Set forth by the clarinets accompanied by the cellos, a diatonic melody in stepwise motion launches the movement and breathes life into the four-bar phrase that contains it. Then the flutes take the lead, articulating a series of descending double thirds in consecutive two-bar phrases along with the other woodwinds. Meanwhile, the accompanying cellos make subtle reference to the arpeggiated motive of the first movement.

An exotic subordinate theme makes a brief appearance, its vaguely Eastern melisma handed over to a solo clarinet before the flutes and remaining woodwinds contribute in unison the slimmest suggestion of a Hungarian dance. The principal theme resurfaces in anticipation of a trio-like new section, in B major. Here the woodwinds outline a jovial theme in consecutive thirds against a periodic descent of the same interval arpeggiated in the strings. Following a return to the principal themes, a brief but peaceful coda brings the movement to a close in a rustic hush of thirds, already savored in the B major section.

Fourth movement: Adagio; Più andante; Allegro non troppo ma con brio

It is no accident that Brahms invests something of the tragic quality of the first movement's introduction in the opening bars of this finale. Rather, it is a compositionally strategic means to bring aesthetic unity to the work. Brahms ushers in the Adagio introduction with considerable solemnity, assigning to the violins a brief but searing melody only two bars long, accompanied by a stream of descending thirds in the woodwinds. Only four and a half bars later, the strings, as if impatient with such an aggrieved expression, contradict the mood in a mysterious staccato interlude that falls under the directive "stringendo" (faster). The effect of this temporary acceleration of tempo is jarring and contrasts sharply with the restatement of the opening material yet again only moments later. The pizzicato motive again interrupts before the introduction of a new motive, played by the woodwinds, that bespeaks urgency in its upward thrust of perfect fifths and fourths. Elsewhere, the violins bow away in an impatient flurry of descending thirty-second-notes.

An abrupt change of key from C minor to C major gives way to a somewhat livelier tempo. A roll of the timpani anticipates the ensuing Più andante, which forms the second half of the introduction. It embraces an expansive new theme as noble as it is enchanting. Borne aloft first by the horns, its expressive refrain is then given over to the flutes, while the strings whisper in tremolos below.

The defining element of the Allegro non troppo, which marks the beginning of the exposition proper, is an ambrosial chorale that Brahms himself implicitly admitted was an homage to Beethoven's "Ode to Joy." "Any ass can see that!" exclaimed an exasperated Brahms to a friend in reaction to a commentary stating as much by the most prominent critic of the day, Eduard Hanslick. No matter that Hanslick intended the remark as a compliment; Brahms was not amused by the idea that such a remark, reprinted again and again in every major newspaper of the time, might be misconstrued and lead to public or even private accusations that he was a plagiarist.

The chorale is tossed from its initial host, the violins, to the horns and flutes and, gaining momentum, is carried aloft by both woodwinds and strings in a resounding *fortissimo* to the bright accompaniment of the trumpets. The violins and bassoons then bellow forth with an energetic torrent of running sixteenth-notes before alighting upon a freshly minted but cheerful subordinate theme in G major, marked "animato" and played by the violins. This theme is distinguished by a sequence of abbreviated phrases, which proceed uniformly from the second (weak) beat of each bar. Two oboes in tandem then pick up the second part of this theme, engaging in a brief but spirited dialogue. But Brahms is not finished yet; he introduces to the symphonic diaspora yet another charismatic tune, one that ascends forcefully in two-note slurs of alternating half- and whole-tone intervals, from C-natural to A-natural. This is vigorously elaborated and intensified for twenty-five bars, by strings and woodwinds, amid a barrage of military triplets.

The chorale returns in the cellos, followed by the woodwinds, but the puckish commentary by the strings playing pizzicato is also reestablished in counterpoint. An energetic fugato drives its point home in a barrage of descending sixteenths alternately buttressed among the violins and the lower strings, before being appropriated by the woodwinds.

An ominous roll of the timpani astride a diminished chord serves to reintroduce the noble horn theme that preceded the exposition, only to find itself combined with the chorale as the timpani fade slowly into the distance. Every one of the principal themes is revisited en route to the coda, which begins rather mysteriously, with a matinal call of horns and strings, again in intervals of thirds and fourths. A magnificent brass-rich march, culminating in a tense rhythm that combines six beats against four in a lively duple meter, launches the work's thrilling conclusion.

Symphony No. 2 in D Major, Op. 73

2 Flutes, 2 Oboes, 2 Clarinets, 2 Bassoons, 4 Horns, 2 Trumpets,
  3 Trombones, 1 Bass Tuba, Timpani, Violins 1 and 2, Violas,
  Cellos, Basses
Composed in 1873 in Portschach on the Worthersee in the
  Austrian Alps
First performance in Vienna, December 30, 1877, with the
  Vienna Philharmonic Orchestra, conducted by Hans Richter

First movement: Allegro non troppo
Second movement: Adagio non troppo
Third movement: Allegretto grazioso (quasi andantino)
Fourth movement: Allegro con spirito

Widely considered the most optimistic of Brahms's symphonies, the elegant and blissful Second has been duly dubbed the "Pastoral." The obvious reference to Beethoven's Sixth Symphony notwithstanding, there is indeed much about the work to recommend that bucolic moniker. Though availing itself of conventional compositional strategies that had long been appropriated in the service of the evocation of nature—the abundant and predominant use of woodwinds, especially French horns and oboes—it is not a work as nearly onomatopoetic as Beethoven's. Indeed, there isn't so much as a single voluminous tremolo in imitation of a thunderstorm, or the peck and call of a cuckoo in the clarinets, anywhere to be found. Instead, Brahms manipulates harmony and rhythm in such a way as to merely suggest the effervescent beauties of nature, making music itself one of them, but on its own terms.

Encouraged by the overwhelming success and public reception of his First Symphony, Brahms resolved to write a second. But this one hardly took twenty years to complete. Indeed, Brahms was done with it in less than a year. His satisfaction expressed itself in his newfound confidence, which he made light of in a memo to his publisher: "The new symphony is so melancholy that you won't be able to stand it. . . . I have never before written anything so sad and mournful." Then, as if to twist the knife, he added, "the score will have to be published with a black border."

Of course the work is not at all mournful. On the contrary, despite the appearance in the second movement of some clouds on its musical horizon, it's an immensely optimistic work, an expression of contentment, serenity, and happiness. The bright tonality of D major plays host to an abundance of musical ideas, which segue effortlessly one into another. The harmonic rhythm—the rate at which harmonies change in a given phrase period—while not unreasonably slow, unfolds gradually, on the whole eschewing huge accents, sudden shifts, innumerable sforzandos, and the compositional violence that these would convey. The profusion of melodies streams by with blithe assurance, for the most part configured, throughout the symphony, in close intervals—that is, in stepwise motion and in thirds. There is something urbane and predictable about Brahms's musically harmonious pasture, but also profoundly affecting.

First movement: Allegro non troppo

The rustic gentility of the opening theme is a musical metaphor of sorts, in that Brahms evokes with unmistakable clarity the dawn of day and a vast expanse. This he does by manipulating instrumental proximity as he exploits the distance between registers. Thus the relatively thin orchestral texture of the opening is in itself suggestive, as if awaiting its turn to blossom into something fuller. The ethereal strains of a high flute, buttressed ever so discreetly by bassoons and clarinets, seem light-years apart from the solemn intonations of the cellos beneath. Add to the mix the incandescent breathiness of horns, which, by the time the violins turn up some seventeen bars into the movement, has become a metaphor for awakening in its own right.

This quiescent introduction quietly evolves, some forty bars later, into a suave second theme whose melodic filigree undulates with uncommon delicacy, first in the violins and then the woodwinds. This is followed by a radiant though slow-moving second theme, chorale-like in its ambience, that emerges dark-hued and is carried forth by the violas and cellos. It brings to mind Brahms's most well-known composition, the "Cradle Song," also known in popular parlance as "Brahms's Lullaby." An emboldened dotted rhythm played in unison by the strings and woodwinds anticipates a vigorous new motive that gallops in a sequence of two sixteenths and an eighth-note. The ensuing response of the strings, led by the cellos, is a particularly warm and expressive motive that angles upward with debonair dispatch.

The development favors the opening theme, from which Brahms fashions a breezy fugato. The trombones, which punctuate the proceedings in imitation, add a distinct edge to the orchestral texture.

The recapitulation commences by combining the first and second themes with such insouciant effortlessness as to blur any line of demarcation between the sections. Brahms is nothing if not generous in his restatement of the exposition's rich materials: witness the array of fluid triplets, played alternately by the violas, which accompany the "chorale" theme, which now finds itself under the command of the oboes, flutes, and clarinets.

The coda is distinguished both by the velvet breath of a French horn, accompanied by the strings, and by the last twenty-seven bars, where both the strings (played pizzicato) and woodwinds engage in a lighthearted staccato dialogue. The horns and trumpets, sustaining a single D for the closing eight bars, fade away in *piano* atop the now nearly vanished strings, and a nearly imperceptible hint of the timpani rumbles, for only a moment, below.

Second movement: Adagio non troppo

The cellos command the lengthy principal theme that introduces this movement, in the key of B major, and do so in a significantly higher register than one would expect to hear. Intoning an ardent yet self-effacing theme over some twelve bars, the cellos disclose, in the first five notes, much about the overall character and trajectory of the entire movement. Indeed, this brief motivic germ, an abbreviated descending scale from F-sharp to B-sharp, sets the stage, as it were, for what is to come. While there is something rather elegiac about its thematic countenance, its mood is not so much solemn and tragic as it is simply resigned. The contrapuntal pull of the accompanying bassoons, which angle upward in the opposite direction with the identical motive, at first appear to contradict the cellos' thematic dominance. But the effect is only momentary, as the cellos elaborate the figure for another ten bars until the violins take over and reiterate the tune.

The horns surface with a wavering eighth-note motive in intervals of thirds and fourths, which is repeated in imitation first by the oboes and flutes. A subtle change of meter from 4/4 to 12/8 gives way to a new theme, a silky barcarole of sorts wherein Brahms integrates woodwinds and strings with seamless panache and deftly sustained hemiolas.

Things intensify as a brief but dense development section gets under way. The prevailing dynamic, a rich piano, suddenly enlarges to forte, and the strings, now burdened with a restless stream of sixteenths, paint a more serious mood in B minor. Here the full orchestra is put to work, as if each instrumental group is determined to have its say.

As both the key and meter revert to their origins, the darker, con-flicted mood of the preceding development dissipates. The principal thematic material is again elaborated by the violins, which express their consternation in the serpentine melisma of close-quartered sixteenths, while the cellos and violas assume the interrogatory counterpoint set forth by the bassoons at the movement's opening.

Third movement: Allegretto grazioso (quasi andantino); Presto ma non assai

In place of the customary scherzo that symphonic tradition might have persuaded Brahms to interject at this point, he instead offers a lilting and ever-so-gracious intermezzo. The ambience is as mercurial as it is bucolic. The violins play no part in the gentle Allegretto, as Brahms entrusts the oboes with the principal melody, a simple, even naive shep-herd's tune harmonized by the clarinets and bassoons and supported by unobtrusive arpeggios played in pizzicato by the cellos below.

On the heels of this woodwind-rich patter, the first of two remarkably agile trios confounds our expectations. For one thing, Brahms
cast it in 2/4 time, a significant metrical shift from the 3/4 that had
prevailed to this point. Two motivic ideas inform this change in meter.
The first is a light-footed, sylvan patter of continuous eighth-notes configured over eight bars as a dialogue between strings and woodwinds.
The second is a brief but forcefully accentuated dotted motive that
articulates its long–short–long pattern with gusto. There is something
Tchaikovskian about this trio, as if the theme itself were an émigré from
the fanciful confections of the Russian kuchkists and their evocation of
troikas, dumkas, and snow.

Following the repetition of the main theme, assigned once again to
the oboes, with the participation of the flutes, a second trio kicks up
its heels in the more conventional meter of three beats to the bar. The
strings inaugurate it with a swift dactylic figure, an ethereal stream
of descending eighth-notes that dances frothily with fleet conviction,
making an ever-so-brief excursion into 9/8 time along the way. If
Brahms had any reason for making that change, which a less gifted
composer would not even have thought of, it was to engender, with
lightning-quick speed, a nearly imperceptible but affectively nuanced
prolongation of the phrase.

The opening theme reappears without fanfare, though now delegated
entirely to the violins. The movement has now come full circle, as it
were, though a brief and exceptionally discreet modulation in the coda
into the remote key of E-flat major invokes an unexpected element of
mystery. As the cellos wind up their supportive arpeggios below, the
flutes and oboes round out the movement with a soulful duet in contrary motion. The clarinets and oboes pipe in with a mere fragment
of the principal tune, bringing this magical movement to its fragile
conclusion.

Fourth movement: Allegro con spirito

Given this movement's symmetrical array of eighth-notes and its frequent sequential repetition of the smallest motivic units, there is an
oddly Mendelssohnian fervor at play here. A breathless four-bar phrase,

played entirely by the strings, launches the work in alla breve time, that is, a rhythmic scenario wherein each measure is divided into two beats rather than four, as the notation (four quarter-notes per bar) otherwise suggests. The pace is swift but not hectic.

A second period of the initial theme, articulated in smaller phrase units, extends the thematic material for another twelve bars. On its heels, the opening theme returns, now fleshed out and expanded by the entire ensemble of instruments. As the flutes, the oboes, and both tiers of violins double up on the principal melody, the cellos, basses, and bassoons keep up the momentum in a run of eighth-notes. The timpani, never far behind, put in their two cents, as well, with a prominent rumble punctuated by sforzandos.

The ambrosial subordinate theme, which in its design is a variant of the principal tune, is carried first by the violas and cellos and then by the flutes. It blossoms with dignity, only to be followed by the full orchestra playing a vigorous descent of quarter-notes. The woodwinds, led by the flutes, assume a joyful whirlwind of ascending and descending thirds, while the strings press on with a flurry of eighth-notes en route to the development.

If there is one place in this movement where there is an overt nature reference, it is in the brief transition from the exposition to the development. The flutes and oboes give way to a playful dotted rhythm that suggests birdsong. But Brahms is quick to reprimand this all-too-brief material, allowing the strings to return with the principal theme. The interjection, in the middle of the development, of a mysterious "tranquillo" also introduces an entirely new chromatic motive that, configured as six notes (two triplets) per bar, is at once tremulous and ambiguous.

The recapitulation ushers itself in with a whisper, giving a platform again, just as it should in classical sonata form, to all of the preceding thematic material, including the double-triplets of the development. The coda, a tensile conduit of all that has come to pass, gives to the trumpets and timpani a certain dominance as they straddle the strings, thus bringing the entire symphony to a joyous, victorious, and altogether brilliant end.

Symphony No. 3 in F Major, Op. 90

2 Flutes, 2 Oboes, 3 Clarinets, 3 Bassoons, 1 Double Bassoon, 4
  Horns, 2 Trumpets, 3 Trombones, 2 Timpani, Violins 1 and 2,
  Violas, Cellos, Basses
Composed in the summer of 1883 at Wiesbaden
First performed on December 2, 1883, by the Vienna
  Philharmonic Orchestra, conducted by Hans Richter

First movement: Allegro con brio
Second movement: Andante
Third movement: Poco allegretto
Fourth movement: Allegro

Brahms was on holiday in Wiesbaden when he set to work on this, the grandest of his four symphonies, in 1883. Given all the horrific news of that lively summer—the eruption of the volcano at Krakatoa that killed more than 36,000 people; the accidental asphyxiation of nearly 200 children at Victoria Concert Hall in London; the sinking at Glasgow of the SS *Daphne,* in which 124 men and boys perished—it's no wonder that Brahms needed to get away. The death of his nemesis, Wagner—who was Moriarty to Brahms's Holmes—must have come as a blow, though there was no love lost there. The passing of Karl Marx occurred that year, although his death probably went entirely unnoticed in Brahms's circles. And one can only wonder if the composer had an opportunity or desire to read Nietzsche's prescient masterpiece, published in 1883, *Also Sprach Zarathustra.*

   Perhaps Brahms's proximity to his new friend the contralto Hermine Spies, inspired him. A more likely candidate for the inspiration behind the Third Symphony, however, was Clara Schumann, with whom Brahms had only a platonic relationship for decades following Robert Schumann's death. Though Clara was the one woman in whom the bachelor Brahms invested his deepest affections, as mentioned previously, theirs was a relationship that was to remain unconsummated. At least that much the often hilarious and wildly inaccurate 1947 film *Song of Love* got right.

Indeed, in lieu of flowers or white chocolates, Brahms sent Clara, on the occasion of her sixty-fourth birthday, the score to the Third Symphony. One can only wonder what Brahms would have sent Georges Sand, had he known her and had similar feelings for her: a cigar, perhaps?

If sometimes a cigar is only a cigar, as Freud is said to have opined, then such an extravagant gift as this (no matter that, in Brahms's mind, its only value was sentimental) was proof enough of his affection. Clara was certainly happy to have it. "I have spent such happy hours with your wonderful creation," she wrote her old friend. "What a poem! From beginning to end one is wrapped about with the mysterious charm of the woods and forests. The second is pure idyll; I can see the worshippers kneeling about the little forest shrine. I hear the babbling brook and the buzz of insects. One's beating heart is soon calmed down again for the final transfiguration which begins with such beauty in the development motive, that words fail me."

While insects would merely annoy most people, Clara embraced the idea of them as a valuable nature metaphor upon which to lavish her highest praise. Not that Brahms didn't deserve it; this symphony is one of his most enthralling works, a model of compositional integrity as well as an emblem of the most profound compassion. There is a humanity about it that sweeps listeners off their feet and into its sonorous bosom. Even a poorly executed performance rarely if ever fails to convey the power of this music or its all-consuming embrace. In a word, it is without question the most charismatic of Brahms's symphonies.

First movement: Allegro con brio (CD Track 1)

The two prolonged and powerful chords that open this hardy Allegro con brio are no mere introduction. In fact, they give shape to the first principal motive, the upper notes of which, F–A–F, again refer to a kind of amalgam (0:01). Though nowhere near as obsessed with such coy epigrammatic references as was his mentor Robert Schumann, it seems Brahms could barely resist the temptation to harvest them where he could. In this case, as in the finale of his F Minor Sonata, F–A–F is an abbreviation for *Frei aber froh* (Free but happy), a motto attributed to Brahms as his response to the *Frei aber einsam* (Free but lonely) motto of his friend and colleague violinist Joseph Joachim. (Never mind that their relationship, strained by Brahms's support for Joachim's wife during particularly messy divorce proceedings, disintegrated until Brahms offered Joachim the opportunity to conduct the second performance of this symphony.) Only three bars into the movement, this truncated fragment returns in the bass, where it is modified with sforzandos in the hope that it will shine through the passionate *forte* of the violins (0:08).

Whether it does or not depends on the efficacy and taste of the conductor, who is also charged with imbuing with life the principal theme, a breathy descent of consecutive two-note slurs awash in anxiety (0:08). Indeed, here Brahms, like virtually every great composer, thinks nothing of appropriating here the sense, if not the letter, of another composer's work, in this case Robert Schumann's. In citing a theme from Schumann's Third Symphony (the "Rhenish"), Brahms pays homage to his mentor and, by proxy, to Clara, too. Legions of thirds and sixths, Brahms's calling card, are entrusted to the violas in pulsating syncopes, which disturb as much as they propel the rhythm— already a mélange that pits duple against triple meters—forward in its inexorable trajectory.

Though firmly entrenched in the absolute-music camp that dismissed Wagner and Liszt as icons of the superficial, Brahms was never able to extricate himself from the influence or at least the musical ubiquity of either. He may not have cared for their music, but he respected them, and, unlike the mean-spirited Wagner, who skewered Brahms with insulting public remarks on more than one occasion, Brahms was careful to avoid such disparagement of his peers.

However, that restraint did not prevent Brahms from taking a potshot or two at Wagner by other, subtler means—that is, in the form of embedded musical references. Musicologist David Brodbeck, in his chapter "Brahms and the New German School" in *Brahms and His World* (Princeton University Press, 1990), points out as much; in the pulsating transitional passage (1:14) to the ardent second subject, Brahms positions a subtle allusion to a passage from the Paris version of Wagner's celebrated

Venusberg music from *Tannhäuser,* to wit, the "Chorus of the Sirens" that wraps up the opera's sinewy Bacchanal. There, the sirens intone

Naht euch dem Strande!	(Approach the strand,
Naht euch dem Lande,	approach the land,
wo in den Armen,	where, in the arms
glühender Liebe	of glowing love,
selig Erwarmen	let blissful warmth
still eure Triebe.	content your desires!)

In Brodbeck's view, which is persuasive, the musical citation (absent the opera's words) is no coincidence, but a deliberate and perhaps tongue-in-cheek reference to the very argument over aesthetics that divided them in the first place. What better way, Brodbeck opines, to undermine Wagner's fragile ego than to invoke the spirited contest, over the meaning of love, between the two singers in *Tannhäuser?*

Intentional or not, the passage is only an allusion, not a duplication of anything specific; Brahms remains his own man, even in bridge passages, and what that passage segues into is one of the symphony's most memorable melodies. Here, a lone clarinet, followed by the strings and then the flutes, sings out a gracious new theme, recast in 9/4 time, assuming its place as the exposition's second subject (1:28). Not to be outdone, the strings close out the exposition at a fever pitch, taking on, with no little drama, a rapidly ascending scale in triplets (2:58). The woodwinds, assigned a lyrical effusion of ascending and descending arpeggios, defeat the demarcation of bar lines through their imposition of our new friend and Brahms's old one, the hemiola (3:12).

The ensuing development pounces upon the second subject of the exposition, making a meal out of it in the cellos and violas (3:27). What had been a gracious and lyrical tune now engorges itself on its own beauty and is transformed into something at once suave and virile. One might even refer to it as a bit of musical machismo, were it not for the feminine dimensions of the slow movement.

A woodwind-rich transitional passage, in a halo of horn calls, anticipates the recapitulation, which is foreshadowed by vague echoes of the principal theme (4:27). The lingering harmonies in this prolonged bridge inform the sudden reentry of the principal theme in toto, tempering its reappearance (5:50) as if by stealth. The irresistible second subject, as suave as ever, makes another welcome nod, though absent the fervor of its earlier incarnation in the development (6:49). The coda, whose entry is announced with a reiteration of the F—A—F motive, now assigned to the horns and trumpets, bursts forth, availing itself of the principal theme with such overwhelming ardor and nervous intensity as to inoculate the listener against any rejection of its considerable charms (8:25). As the movement draws to a close, Brahms shuns any hint of bravado, instead allowing the work to fade away, quiescent and self-satisfied.

Second movement: Andante

The dawn of this discreet Andante in rondo form is a hushed chorale set forth by the woodwinds. Significantly, as we shall see, the key is C major. Here the clarinets and bassoons sing with pious humility, only to be met with the restrained response of the violas, cellos, and bass. A subtle reference to the F—A—F (*Frei aber froh*) motive of the first movement materializes briefly as the clarinets come to a cadence only twenty-one bars into the movement. Then a new melody, cast in a gentle spiral of ascending sixteenth-notes and enlivened first by the oboes and then the flutes, sets sail on the musical horizon. Gaining confidence, it lifts the veil of solace that informed the opening measures. The violins, as is their wont, boldly assume this same melodic strand, proclaiming it brightly and with the best of intentions.

Suddenly, the mood darkens, and the violins and violas, segregated in unison and in pizzicato, are thrown into relief without support from any other instruments, save for the muffled accompaniment of the cellos and basses. They sound meek and submissive, almost as if Brahms demands they atone for their sins.

Though I have yet to read even so much as a single analysis of this movement that takes notice, the ensuing theme—the new thematic kid on the block—adumbrates Debussy in more ways than one. The simple melody assumed by the clarinet could be a distant cousin, or at least the motivic element, that informed if not inspired the thematic material that opens the French composer's languid opera, *Pelléas et Mélisande*.

Following the violins and woodwinds, which enter into a dialogue with a subtle elaboration of the foregoing theme, a particularly haunting transitional passage slows the movement to a crawl. Repeated note couplets pulsate delicately with the assured serenity of an ocean tide responding to the gravitational pull of the moon. Then, in tandem with the violins, which ebb and flow in a lush stream of hemiolas, a variant of the principal theme returns, embodied by the cellos and bassoons. Dynamics intensify in a swell of hairpin crescendos and diminuendos before the reemergence of the sixteenth-note spiral, again in the violins, that informed the movement's opening section. The woodwinds return with the principal theme, accompanied by the strings, which pass the sixteenth-note motivic fragment among themselves with quiet resignation.

The coda takes its once-in-a-movement opportunity to survey its motivic progeny one last time, breaking the news with a heart-wrenching plea that spans only a moment. Then, just as certainly as they had beckoned us in the first place, the compositional lights dim, and all their exquisite beauties, having been recollected one last time, vanish forlorn into the musical distance.

Third movement: Poco allegretto

It is no accident that Brahms chose C minor as the home key of this Poco allegretto. It is the parallel minor of C major, the key in which the just-concluded Andante was cast. By linking these two closely related keys within the same tonal ethos (both spring from the dominant of F major, the principal key of the symphony), Brahms buttresses continuity, prolonging the overall arc of tension, which on some unconscious level heightens our sense of expectation and inspires a yearning for resolution, that is, for a return to the "home," or tonic, key.

Key relationships, whether in the micro or in the macro, have this power to stimulate our listening organism toward and away from key centers, whether we know it or not. Anyone who has been interrupted while humming even the most innocuous familiar tune, be it "Happy Birthday" or "Auld Lang Syne," knows well this feeling of defeat and frustration, at least in musical terms.

In the opening theme, one of Brahms's most endearing, the cellos, only slimly accompanied by the other strings, flutes, and bassoons, sing out with plaintive regret, giving body to a kind of mournful soliloquy in search of company. In the context of Brahms's symphonic output, it's an unusually long melody, and though deftly articulated in two-bar phrases and two-note slurs, it extends over fifteen bars in a continuous bel canto–like legato. The violins are not far behind, inscribing themselves impatiently into the melody only moments before the cellos have concluded their business. This discreet dovetailing is as fluid as it ingenious, at least in architectural categories: this movement, like the Andante before it, is a rondo, wherein the periodic return of thematic material frames an abundance of new, subsidiary themes. The nearly imperceptible materialization of a theme is akin to a photographic emulsion, which, when developed in a chemical solution, comes gradually and mysteriously into view.

The orchestral texture continues to favor the strings until the flutes and oboes appoint themselves heir, only a few moments later, to the same thematic material. The key signature changes to four flats, throwing the movement into A-flat major and giving birth to a lilting new theme given over to the woodwinds, with the flutes and clarinets at the helm and in unison. Recalling the oscillating midsection duet of the F Minor Piano Sonata, it's a delicate tune that proceeds in a consecutive stream of two-note slurs, drawn over the bar lines, thus creating what might be called, quite literally, an upbeat character. The charm of their effect is enhanced by the quiet accompaniment of the cellos, whose playful and coquettish arpeggiations ascend and descend in brief staccato spurts.

Soon enough, the key signature migrates back to C minor. Restored to its rightful place, this predominant tonality again plays host to the principal theme, now given over to the horns, which look after it with all the tenderness of a doe tending her fawns. (Gives a whole new meaning to *do re mi,* doesn't it?)

The all-too-brief coda, only fourteen bars long, expresses its longing in hemiola rhythm, tying elongated quarter-notes, each modified by a hairpin crescendo/decrescendo swell, over the bar lines. The entire orchestra, resigned to a sadness of its own creation, makes one last gasp and ascends in a slow dotted rhythm to a high B-flat before evaporating altogether into the hazy shadow of C minor.

Fourth movement: Allegro

The mysterious, rather sultry thematic stream that defines the opening theme of this movement proceeds with a certain caution, as if wary of what might be coming next. Carried forward by the strings and bassoons in unison, it presides comfortably over its own rumblings, until arrested by a contrasting theme, a halting pulsation in half-notes and triplets. On its heels is a vigorous dotted figure, which, energized by the woodwinds and brass, returns sheepishly to the opening theme, if only for a moment. Once there, it is again borne aloft in *pianissimo* by the violas and cellos. But the dotted figure will have none of it; it imposes itself again en route to a new and wholly confident second theme, spun out by the cellos and horns in quarter-note triplets. While the rhythm here is complex—it pits these triplets against an accompaniment in duple meter played by the bassoons and basses, as well as a faster group of eighth-note triplets in the violins and violas—it is also entirely characteristic of Brahms. This metrical displacement engenders a kind of persistent, offbeat inner motor that compels the music forward, creating in its wake what the Germans call *Schwung,* or "swing." It's an irresistible rhythm that gets just as much into one's hips and guts as does a Brazilian samba on a sweaty day in Rio.

Tensions mount as the violins and woodwinds grab on to a marchlike thematic fragment that boasts a strong accent on the weak second beat on each of the four bars that constitute it. The principal theme resurfaces quietly in the woodwinds, only to be detoured by a brief fugato, which passes by with the insouciance of an afterthought. An excursion into an army of triplets, presided over by the strings in contrary and parallel motion, stirs things up considerably. The entire array of themes introduced in the first pages of the movement reveals itself yet again, until the second theme, now attenuated, exhausted and entrusted to the muted violas, peers timorously through the thin veneer of a burgeoning coda. The woodwinds, led by the flutes, amble along in thirds as they breathe life into a variant of the principal theme. As the basses alight on open fifths—a muffled cry from their sepulchral register—the violins and violas shimmer in a quiet halo of running sixteenth-notes that, configured as a slow trill, bathe the symphony's conclusion in a pale light. A vague echo of the first movement's principal theme comes fleetingly into view but, set forth in this diaphanous gauze, enshrines itself as both a distant memory and a final farewell.

Symphony No. 4 in E Minor, Op. 98

*2 Flutes, 2 Oboes, 2 Clarinets, 4 Horns, 2 Trumpets,
   3 Trombones, Timpani, Triangle, Violins 1 and 2, Violas,
   Cellos, Basses*
Composed 1884–85
*Premiere on October 25, 1885, in Meiningen, conducted by
   Brahms*

First movement: Allegro non troppo
Second movement: Andante moderato
Third movement: Allegro giocoso
Fourth movement: Allegro energico e passionate

That a composer of Brahms's stature managed almost invariably to compose his greatest works while on "on vacation" is remarkable. One can only wonder what the notion of vacation could have meant to a man whose entire life was consumed by the creative process and the assorted intellectual pursuits that went along with it. The Fourth Symphony has its origins in the district of Mürzzuschlag in Styria, an area of southeastern Austria that borders on Slovenia. Evidently, the sun and mountain air put the composer in good spirits, engendering the wit for which he was famous. Certainly, Brahms could be glib about his work and even self-deprecating: "God forbid, it's nothing so aristocratic," he opined about his Fourth Symphony. Indeed, in this letter to his friend Max Kalbeck, he joked that the entire symphony was nothing but "another collection of polkas and waltzes."

   Today, of course, we know this work, the last of his outings in the symphonic genre, to be a great deal more than that. Of all the symphonies, it stands out as the apotheosis of his compositional mastery, a model of economy in which all of the varied elements of his style coalesce. Though Brahms's embrace of classicism struck his antagonists, not the least of whom were Liszt and Wagner, as anachronistic, the fact remains that in just as many ways he anticipated the compositional innovations of the twentieth century. After Beethoven, no one wrote as many sets of variations as Brahms, nor invigorated the form with greater imagination and gusto. The ascent of serial variations, for example, to the status of an aesthetic totem in the music of Schoenberg, Berg, Zemlinsky, and other major composers of the twentieth century would likely have been unimaginable without him.

Though he still had some fourteen years of life left in him, Brahms would never compose another symphony after this one. He destroyed the sketches he made for a Fifth, preserving only a few elements for his String Quartet Op. 111. Perhaps that is why he not-so-jokingly referred to the Fourth as his "neue traurige Symphonie" ("new sad symphony").

First movement: Allegro non troppo

In an uncharacteristic move, Brahms launches the Fourth Symphony without any fanfare. There is no introduction, and significantly, he jettisoned from his original sketches two introductory bars that were to have been played by the woodwinds. Save for the barely bleating accompaniment of the winds, here the strings assume all responsibility, giving way to a graceful and lyrical effusion that is to follow. Supported by a light ascent of arpeggios in the lower strings, the violins take immediate possession of the principal melody, a dulcet but somewhat mournful refrain set in a procession of falling thirds and ascending sixths, arranged in slurred couplets wherein the unaccented tone occurs on the downbeat. Each of these couplets, in turn, is punctuated midbar by quarter-rests.

Providing the conductor pays more attention to "non troppo," than to "allegro," the effect, is somewhat unsettling, especially in the context of the velvety hush that allows quiescence to reign.

Certainly, there is good reason, in the music of Brahms, that a procession of falling thirds, organized in sequence as they are here, should disturb the listener's expectations. Indeed, Brahms had long since appropriated this motivic figure as an expressive systole in his compositional vocabulary. But expressive of what? Well, scholars have long held that Brahms associated falling thirds with death, pointing out other instances of their occurrence in his music, not the least of which are several of his songs where death is the subject, among them "Feldeinsamkeit" (Op. 86, No. 2), "Mit vierzig Jahren" (Op. 94, No. 1), "Der Tod, das ist die kühle Nacht" (Op. 96, No. 1), and "O Tod" (from the *Vier Ernste Gesänge*, Op. 121). *A German Requiem*, too, has its share of descending thirds. Thus the Fourth Symphony augurs eerily what might be construed to be Brahms's sense of his own mortality more than a decade before his own passing. Perhaps he knew, or at least resolved in some private or perhaps unconscious way, that the Fourth would be his last symphony.

The second period of the principal theme, which already begins to modulate to a remote key, avails itself of octave leaps as it obliterates the grammar of the rests. A string of descending scales dovetails among the woodwinds as the violins mimic the rhythm of the opening's falling thirds but now do so in octaves. Suddenly, and with unexpected fervor, the winds, buttressed by an edgy trumpet, bellow forth in *forte* with a bold marchlike motive, introducing the movement's subsidiary thematic material. Embedded within this motive are two sixteenth-notes followed by a triplet, lending the figure a somewhat strident character. But this quality is tempered only a few bars later by the cellos and then the violins, which bring forth a new melodic fragment. Provided with a lively dotted-note accompaniment in pizzicato played by violas and basses, this exotic theme bears all the earmarks of a Magyar folk song. Yet more thematic material makes itself known, first with the flutes, which introduce an abbreviated descending scale in thirds, and then the violins, which elaborate that idea. Indeed, the violins here have their moment. As this seemingly innocuous motivic fragment passes from the woodwinds to the violins, which sing it out ardently from the bright summit of a high B, the change of orchestral color is so vivid as to suggest the emergence of the sun from behind a patch of winter clouds. The effect of this passage is visceral, as if the music, leaping off the page, has assumed human form and embraced its listener. A dialogue ensues between the woodwinds, playing the fanfare motive, and the strings, which are assigned a mysterious arpeggio in *pianissimo.*

The development is a playful affair, giving voice to every motivic strand that has informed the movement thus far. A variant of the scalar design that informed the closing of the exposition becomes a gentle dialogue between woodwinds and strings, but not before the woodwinds, over the whispered rumble of the timpani, quietly appropriate the exposition's second theme, expanding its triplet configuration in an airy tumble of motivic fragments. In anticipation of the recapitulation, the woodwinds and strings engage in a gracious conversation, tossing between themselves the lyrical second period of the principal theme. The recapitulation recaptures the foregoing, raising the stakes by allowing the horns and trombones a prominence. As if in an effort to save its resources, the orchestral texture thins as the string of motivic fragments fades into an ethereal *ppp* (*pianississimo*).

A lengthy coda pays tribute to the characteristic triplets of the second theme, where the woodwinds take over astride the defiant calls of the trumpet and horns. The strings reclaim the principal thematic material they once owned, harvesting it anew but now transforming it, in the context of a robust *fortissimo,* into something granitic and defiant. Brahms keeps the strings busy in pursuit of their engagement of an alternating array of dominant–tonic chords that bring the movement to its heroic close.

Second movement: Andante moderato

The simple melody in 6/8 time that sets this movement in motion positions itself in stark contrast to the drama of the Allegro moderato. The horns introduce this stoic introduction, a gentle but persistent reiteration of repeated notes articulated by a dotted rhythm in sixteenths. It takes only one measure before the figure is consumed whole by the woodwinds. The serene mood engendered by the melody's heartbeat rhythm is further enhanced by the strings, which have been temporarily relegated to a barely audible pizzicato accompaniment. The clarinets give shape to the principal theme, which proves to be only a slight variant of the horns' introduction. The violins then sink their teeth into the motive but reject it only a few bars later in favor of a broad and affecting new melodic strand. Here Brahms establishes a rhythmic configuration characteristic of his compositional vocabulary, to wit, a duple meter in tandem with a triple meter. Indeed, the violas, assigned a river of sixteenth-note triplets, create a sensuous undercurrent.

Only seven bars later, a transitional passage engages the winds and strings in a vigorous dialogue that serves as a transitional passage to a tender new melody, in stepwise motion, carried aloft by the cellos. A diaphanous cascade enshrouds the return of the principal theme, now a dulcet memory set forth by the violins, but not for long. Taking it to a higher register, the strings, in both unison and contrary motion, elaborate the principal theme with a flurry of thirty-second-note arpeggios in unison, making way for the return of the expressive secondary theme in stepwise motion. Now entrusted to the violins, the expressive secondary theme in stepwise motion returns, gaining momentum and intensity in syncopation.

Beethoven is again the inspiration for the coda. As Kenneth Hull observes in his "Allusive Irony in Brahms's Fourth Symphony," Brahms alludes to the famous noble theme in C major that Beethoven used no fewer than three times in the Andante con moto of his no-less-famous Fifth Symphony. Even the instrumentation is similar, as clarinets are the bearers of the theme in both works. In the Brahms, an oboe complements the clarinets as the theme presides over a sustained B-natural in the timpani, cellos, and bass, while in Beethoven, the violins do the same. The movement draws to its conclusion with clarinets and horns, which are again awash in the noble strains of the principal theme.

Third movement: Allegro giocoso

As Brahms himself put it, "three kettledrums, triangle, and piccolo will, of course, make something of a show." Indeed they do in this brusque and ebullient confection in C major. The exposition's opening theme, a truncated descending scale pattern in 2/4 time, is distinguished by its unusual articulation. Of the four eighth-notes that make up its first and third bars, the second and third of them fall under a slur. As this configuration gives greater emphasis to the weak beat in the bar, it tends to unsettle the natural accentuation, which would favor the strong beat.

Despite the meter (and despite the movement being in sonata form), there is something Beethovenian about the overall character and ambience of this Allegro giocoso. For example, the sudden descent in the fifth bar, from an E-natural to a heavily accented A-natural almost two octaves lower, is perhaps a reference to the scherzo of Beethoven's Fourth, which boasts a similar effect. This is followed by a nervous anapest—a brief sequence of two staccato sixteenth-notes followed by an eighth, and then by four slurred sixteenths—that sprints across the bar lines and makes itself known. While strings jockey for dominance often here, subsequently busying themselves in a driving flurry of sixteenths, the winds are never far behind.

The full orchestra overtakes a brief fanfare, giving particular prominence to a motivic strand configured as a triplet followed by two quarter-notes, the second of which, also on a weak beat, is modified with a biting accent. The piccolo brightens the compositional day as a playful second theme, taken up by the violins and not so jittery as the principal one, makes its rounds.

That terse development section avails itself of the thematic material, reinventing it as a no-less-energetic systole, but this time in A minor. The recapitulation offers a few surprises, not the least of which is its *pianissimo* restatement of the principal thematic material in the woodwinds; the mischievous aggression of the opening has all but vanished this time around. The tempo briefly pulls back in "poco meno presto," as the horns and oboes sketch a bucolic new fragment that echoes the second theme of the first movement. As the timpani assume the anapest motive with quiet determination, a lively coda presses forward, combining the various themes as it comes to its joyful conclusion.

Fourth movement: Allegro energico e passionate

The eight-bar introduction to this unusual finale is not an introduction at all, but the theme (ostinato) that forms the basis for a passacaglia, that is, a string of uninterrupted variations over a recurring bass line. The complexity of this movement, though, proceeds not only from the variations but also from the superimposition of sonata form over its thirty-four variations.

The opening salvo, assigned to the woodwinds with the rich and vociferous support of the trombones and horns below, sets forth the principal ostinato as an abbreviated minor scale with the addition of an alien pitch, A-sharp, the raised fourth degree of the scale. This theme has been attributed to the finale of Bach's Cantata No. 150, *Nach dir, Herr, verlanget mich* (I yearn for you, O Lord), the text of which reads like a consolation:

> I spend my days in sorrow,
> Yet God ends them in joy;
> Christians on the thorny path
> Heaven leads with strength and blessing;
> God remains my faithful treasure
> So I heed not mortal suffering.
> Christ, who stands at our side,
> Helps me daily to strive triumphantly.

There, Bach's text expresses an unwavering faith in God that, in Christian theology, presumes that death is nothing to fear but rather should be welcomed for the eternal happiness it promises.

However, it is also possible to discern within Brahms's ostinato a subtle reference to the last movement of Beethoven's "Eroica" Symphony, a set of variations that Beethoven also used in *Creatures of Prometheus*. Constituting the kernel of the "Eroica" theme (which coincidentally also fills out an eight-bar phrase) are two notes, E-flat–B-flat, which are repeated in inversion over four bars. (The motive thus formed is E-flat–B-flat–B-flat–E-flat.) While Brahms has indeed embedded those identical notes in the principal theme of this movement (albeit in reverse order, and not consecutively), it may be more than coincidence. Beethoven also availed himself of the raised fourth degree of the scale as the penultimate pitch in his theme. As we have seen, Brahms's discreet allusion to Wagner's Venusberg music in the Third Symphony lent that work a certain metaphorical quality, while in the First Symphony he cited, by his own admission, Beethoven's "Ode to Joy." Beethoven was again the source of Brahms's pleasure when, in his First Piano Sonata, he blatantly quoted the principal motive of the "Hammerklavier" Sonata, Op. 106, though in that case its status as an allusion is questionable. There the young Brahms seems less intent in using music for critical commentary than in paying homage to the man he viewed as the greatest composer of the nineteenth century.

Even so, while it may be reasonable to suppose that in this case Brahms appropriated the "Eroica" (Prometheus) theme as a kind of homage, there may be more to it than that. Prometheus's gift to humanity was fire, or the "divine spark," and that in turn is a metaphor for resistance and change. The Promethean myth, then, is not overwhelmed by the idea of death but, on the contrary, is life-affirming. As we have seen, even the finale of the Bach Cantata No. 150 yields to triumph over tragedy, inviting parallels with the Prometheus legend.

The first few variations are sparse, given over to the woodwinds, until the fourth, fifth, and sixth variations give way to a lush theme of yearning, assumed by the violins. The seventh variation, which bears some relation, at least in rhythmic design, to the principal theme of the first movement, empties out into an uneasy profusion of sixteenths. The meter changes to 3/2 as a lone flute sings out a sad soliloquy. In the following three variations, the horns offer a slow and solemn consolation before the restatement of the principal theme. Now something on the order of a development section begins. Tensions mount as the thematic material woven around the theme assumes urgency that until now it did not have. Violin tremolos, a jaunty staccato figure, accentuated triplets, and unabashed bursts of the trombone inform the next eleven variations. The mood relaxes in the twenty-seventh and twenty-eighth variations, wherein a gracious melody, played in thirds and in unison by the flutes, clarinets, and bassoons, rides astride an easygoing stream of triplets played in contrary motion by the violins and violas.

A new tempo marking, più allegro, picks up the pace as it informs the final four variations. These in turn form the movement's brisk coda, which once again gives sanctuary to the principal theme. For the last time the woodwinds assert their proprietorship, proudly proclaiming the theme as their own, over the evident objection of the bellicose arpeggios strung along by the violins below. With slurs and uncompromising accentuations on every beat in every bar, the movement draws to its magnificent conclusion and, in so doing, brings Brahms's career as a symphonist to a glorious end.

The Piano Music

I n 1873 Brahms complained to his publisher Fritz Simrock, who was growing impatient for the manuscript of the First Symphony, that living and composing in the shadow of Beethoven was intimidating. "I will *never* write another symphony," he gnarled. "You don't know what it means to the likes of us, when we hear his footsteps behind us!"

Certainly, in comparison to Beethoven and Liszt, Brahms cannot properly be described as a prolific composer for the piano. Though well known for his compositionally conservative agenda and as a devotee of classicism, he declined to write dozens of pianos sonatas, as did Mozart, Beethoven, and Haydn, preferring instead to throw his energy into smaller forms: intermezzos, ballades, scherzos, rhapsodies, and variations. Indeed, he abandoned the piano sonata as a formal receptacle early on, following the publication of his Sonata in F Minor, Op. 5, a work that might best be interpreted as a symphony in the form of a piano piece. What's more, he stopped writing piano music altogether shortly after his arrival in Vienna in 1862. Indeed, with the exception of his Waltzes in 1865, he declared a self-imposed moratorium on piano composition until 1879, the year that saw the publication of his Two Rhapsodies, Op. 79.

Brahms rejected the idea of program music, a position that cost him dearly early on in his career, when he publicly disparaged, in an ill-advised manifesto, the musical-dramatic agenda exemplified by Liszt (and thus, by implication, by Wagner). Though Brahms had gathered some twenty prominent musicians to sign the document, only three names were affixed, including his own, Hanslick's, and Joachim's, thanks to a snafu that led to its premature publication in the German press. Even so, it should be noted that the source of Wagner's hostility toward Brahms, whom he hardly knew, proceeded less from their philosophical differences than it did from the relationship each had with Mathilde von Wesendonck, a wealthy aristocrat who had for some time been both Wagner's mistress and patron. By 1861, Brahms had become, in Wesendonck's eyes, the more esteemed artistic presence, and she lavished on him every ounce of her largesse; at the same time, she marginalized Wagner, denied him a much-needed loan, and finally flat-out refused him entry to her home.

With professional and personal jealousy governing the day, Wagner did not exactly have warm feelings for Brahms, either. Brahms's embrace of so-called absolute music evolved from his disinclination to see any determinative value in creating music that could in any way be construed as dependent on poetry and drama. For Brahms, it was always the immanent content of a composition that mattered, and he trusted it would convey, on strictly compositional terms, its own wordless, spiritual message. Embracing abstraction as the meat and potatoes of compositional integrity, Brahms just went his way, while Wagner and his devotees went theirs.

The miniature piano pieces that make up Opuses 116, 117, 118, and 119 best exemplify Brahms's avuncular disposition. This collection of capriccios, intermezzi, romances, and ballades breathes gemütlichkeit, as it eschews the superficial, making its points not through the imposition of blazing arpeggios, thundering octaves, resilient roulades, and stentorian rhetoric, but through more private, understated means. While intimacy lost nothing of its implicit sensuality in the piano music of Brahms—especially in the late music—it declined to proclaim its sentiments or to wear them on its sleeve. On the contrary, each work in these suites is a model of compositional economy, giving voice to its ideas by turning declamation on its head. Here, in any one of these remarkable pieces, Brahms proves himself nothing if not exceptionally resourceful. Even the smallest motivic germ becomes an occasion for contemplation, variance, quiescent manipulation, and contrapuntal probity.

The titles attached to his late piano music are largely fanciful; in spite of his musical conservatism and his penchant for classical decorum, Brahms was never one to be pigeonholed strictly by formal considerations. His richly polyphonic sensibility, along with his fierce determination to elaborate and vary thematic material as it unfolded, drove him to reinvent traditional forms more than it compelled him to create new ones.

Let me step back for a moment to have a brief, though necessarily superficial, look at the division that acted as a stake driven through the heart of musical aesthetics during Brahms's lifetime and continues to do so today. I refer to that century-and-a-half-old polemic pitting absolute music against program music (or against any composition or composer that dares to extol the artistic role that language, drama, and poetry might play in music). It was precisely this polemic that was at the heart of the aforementioned manifesto. It is also an argument that has hardly abated, and while I fail to see any point in arguing about the value of Brahms's piano music in comparison to Liszt's (or anyone else's, for that matter), the issue can't be ignored, either. After all, there are those who, even today, see nothing more in the music of Liszt than superficial display, the innovations of his compositional vocabulary be damned. While any perception of that kind, no matter how naive, can be attributed in part to poorly executed performances by less-than-savvy musicians, it is also an argument that conveniently ignores equally important matters.

There is neither parity nor any need for it in the household of compositional agenda. Where authoritative, committed, and ingenious composers such as Liszt and Wagner are concerned, there doesn't have to be. Certainly, their music, which is no less original than that of Brahms, is complex and, whatever the means of expression, purposeful. The notion set forth by Brahms's supporters and Liszt's antagonists, that the latter was somehow inferior to the former, remains stillborn, as there is no point in fashioning a homology that could substantively link the works and artistic ideals of these composers, rendering their individual compositional vocabularies equal. While it is indeed useful and instructive to come to general terms with the overall rift that, in the nineteenth century, divided one aesthetically inclined "camp" from another, to pit Liszt and Wagner against Brahms and Schumann amounts to little more than an exercise in gaining the upper hand in an exclusive society of equals. The music of any composer, regardless of stature, ought ideally be able to satisfy its own concept, whatever that may be. Academic sparring that avails itself in its own defense of clever, deftly drafted, and rigorous technical analysis will do nothing to affect the message, integrity, or power of great music. Which leaves only the question: What is great music?

As that is not for me to answer, nor within the scope of this book, I'll parry that one, at least for the time being. What does concern us here is Brahms's piano music, which is abundant enough in every category. While it is possible to discern common threads that tie his early to his late piano music—a preoccupation, for example, with double thirds and sixths, hemiolas, cross-rhythms, Gypsy music, frequent imitation, complex polyphony, and powerful sonorities that swell up wavelike from the bass and recede in the most quiescent *pianissimos*—such generalized phenomena are nowhere near as fascinating as those that a pianist, as much as the listener, would be well rewarded to localize in the particular.

Of course, it has become de rigueur in musicological circles to divide every composer's lifespan and career into periods, without convincingly distinguishing a specific temporal demarcation that can lay claim to one work belonging to this period or that one. It is merely a truism that Brahms's three piano sonatas, Opuses 1, 2, and 5, the Scherzo Op. 4, and the Ballades Op. 10, composed between 1851 and 1854, are products of his youth, and that the aforementioned miniatures (Opuses 116, 117, 118, and 119) are the autumnal confections of his old age. A segue in time (1855–76) to the Waltzes, Op. 39 (1865), several sets of variations (Op. 21, 24, and the Paganini Variations, Op. 35), and the Two Rhapsodies, Op. 79 (1879) shows no lessening of his creativity, though these works do paint their composer as one whose austerity gained ground the older he got.

Any discussion of Brahms's music, be it critical or glib, encounters certain extramusical problems, owing to the neurotic perfectionism that often compelled him to destroy his work. As mentioned earlier, if the least dissatisfied, Brahms thought nothing of starting over again from scratch or returning to his sketches, or even to a completed composition, to make additional modifications. He rejected the original slow movement of the First Symphony, replacing it after the first few performances with the Adagio that we have come to know and love today. If unhappy with the final form of a work he otherwise approved, he would change the medium. For example, the first incarnation of what is now the F Minor Piano Quintet, Op. 34, did not include a piano at all; it was a string quintet. Terrified of producing, much less making public, anything that failed to meet his rigorous standards, he refused to compromise his principles. To that end, he took Joachim's harsh criticism of the Quintet to heart; he recast it with a piano. Clara Schumann, too, expressed her icy resistance to the idea of adding a piano, having lavished effusive praise upon hearing the original version for strings.

Regrettably, I cannot survey, in these few pages, all of Brahms's piano music. While that may be possible in future, I have for the time being selected only certain major works, from each phase of his long life, for evaluation.

Sonata No. 3 in F Minor, Op. 5

Dedicated to Frau Gräfin von Hohenthal

First movement: Allegro maestoso
Second movement: Andante
Third movement: Scherzo; Allegro energico
Fourth movement: Intermezzo (Rückblick); Andante molto
Fifth movement: Finale; Allegro moderato ma rubato

Brahms wrote only three piano sonatas, all of them early on in his career. As we have already observed, he became disenchanted with the genre, preferring to turn his attention to symphonic and chamber music, as well as lieder. Each of the sonatas is monumental in concept as well as substance, leaving me room, in this modest volume, to take a look at only one of them, the F Minor, in detail. He actually completed what is now called his First Sonata, in C Major, *after* he wrote the Second Sonata (in F-sharp Minor, Op. 2). Having convinced himself the C Major was the better of the two, he had it published as his Opus 1.

No matter the chronology, the First Sonata is a remarkable creation for a composer of Brahms's years; he was not even twenty when he wrote it. The work is abundant in allusions both musical and literary: to Beethoven's "Hammerklavier" Sonata, Op. 106; to Schubert's "Wanderer Fantasy"; and to the Scottish bard Robert Burns. Why he took a dimmer view of his ebullient F-sharp Minor Sonata is puzzling; it's an electrifying work, yet even today it is rarely performed.

The F Minor Sonata, composed when Brahms was barely twenty-one, is symphonic in scope, To be sure, it was around this time that Brahms contemplated the composition of a symphony and began to sketch one out. But the project fizzled. Still uncomfortable in his own skin, he set aside his ideas for several years, only to harvest them later for use in other works, including the D Minor Piano Concerto.

The F Minor Sonata comprises five, rather than four, movements, thus enlarging its scope considerably. Though some have interpreted its poignant Intermezzo as merely transitional, it is in fact an entirely autonomous movement that elaborates one of the sonata's defining motives. It is a motive that Brahms returns to again and again and that is a clear reference, as we shall see, to the famous opening salvo of Beethoven's Fifth Symphony.

The composition of this sonata was not of a piece. On holiday along the Rhine when he wrote it in the summer of 1853, Brahms penned the Andante and Intermezzo movements first. Shortly thereafter, on September 30 of that same year, with a recommendation from Joachim in hand, he met Robert and Clara Schumann. He completed the sonata while in residence at their home, submitting it to Schumann for his critical assessment.

First movement: Allegro maestoso

The opening movement, a vigorous Allegro maestoso in 3/4 time, exploits the full range of the piano. The opening bar introduces the principal motive, a fierce, ascending, chord-encased dotted motive that is buttressed in the bass by the chromatic descent, on the first beat of each of the next five bars, of strongly accentuated octaves. Oddly enough, the actual motivic germ is concealed in all this bluster;

what it amounts to is only four notes, the first three configured in descending stepwise motion before ascending by a whole tone to its final note. Rhythmically they form a string of note values configured as long–short–short–long. On the heels of a brusque cadence on a C major chord (the dominant of F minor), a new, succinctly articulated chordal theme, alternating a tonic chord with an altered subdominant, emerges in the tenor, accompanied in the bass by an ominous rumble of open fifths, configured as triplets in imitation of timpani. A flurry of octaves reestablishes and expands the opening salvo en route to a marchlike transitional (or bridge) passage, which is likewise configured as a strident succession of chords in emulation of trumpets. "Fest und bestimmt" (strong and determined) is the pertinent instruction that informs this passage.

The second theme, marked "con espressione," is a barometer of the great symphonist Brahms would later become. Hovering over a stream of continuous, widely spaced eighth-notes is a lush and ardent melody set in counterpoint to a discretely slurred alto voice. Here he attempts to evoke the strains of a bow gliding across the strings of a violin. The bass, too, suggests the gentle tug of the cellos and violas against the principal melody's charismatic tide. An accelerando modifies the second half of this motive, which Brahms relocates from the middle of the piano to its soprano register.

The brief development focuses on the opening themes of the exposition, transforming them dynamically from a robust *forte* to the thinnest *pianissimo*. Combining the pulsating timpani motive, now displaced into treble, with the opening dotted figure, now grumbling gruffly in the bass, Brahms proves he is not one who cares to be misinterpreted. He plainly indicates "misterioso" as the prevailing mood. But that mood changes quickly, as the themes bellow forth in a cumulative crescendo. Ignoring the conventions of sonata form, the audacious young Brahms, perhaps to prove a point, declines to include, at the onset of the recapitulation, the principal material of the exposition. Changing the key to F major, Brahms instead commences with the transitional passage in advance of reintroducing the tender second theme.

As Eric Le Van has shrewdly observed, this movement parts company with the compositional strategies of Liszt and his protagonists, in that Brahms reinvents the concept of thematic transformation, that Rosetta stone of romantic-era aesthetics.

> Such architectonic procedures (only timidly tried out in the two preceding sonatas) on first glance appear to draw Brahms into the fold of the Lisztians and proponents of the "New German School": the principal technique Lisztians were most fond of consisted in the transformation of a given theme under different aspects. Whereas the Lisztian principle demands an all-out abandonment of sonata-allegro form in favour of an essentially rhythmical per-mutation of various thematic ideas, Brahms employs a cyclical technique only within the framework of sonata-allegro form, and applies this technique solely to principal subjects.

This leads me to bring up an important point with regard to the performance of this massive sonata. An informed pianist is one who has taken the trouble to study Brahms's orchestral and choral works, with a view toward understanding not only what Brahms had in mind, but what he had in his ear. Here, savvy interpreters will put their imagina-tion to work to distinguish the overall timbre of the first entry of this lovely theme from its second. While there are innumerable ways for a pianist to convey a difference in sound quality (this can be effected, for example, by depressing the keys from a position just below the key bed, or brightening the sound by approaching them from above, or using the damper, sostenuto, and una corda pedals in varying combinations, to name only a few possible solutions), the point is to translate the rather limited sonority of the piano into something approximating the sound of orchestral instruments. Had this been an orchestral work, Brahms might well have assigned the subsequent incarnation of the second theme to the oboes or clarinets; or he might have organized them in that very combination the first time around. Ultimately it is up to the informed taste of the player to make that decision and carry it through consistently.

In the coda, Brahms at last revisits verbatim the work's opening material. In doing so at this point, he has in effect turned the very idea of recapitulation on its head. When he writes "più animato," as he does some eighteen bars from the end, he means it; a series of massive chords in couplets again spans the full range of the keyboard, blazing forth Beethoven-like from a bellowing *forte* to a murmuring *piano*. A short excursion into 5/4 time accelerates the rhythm and intensifies the trajectory, bringing the movement to a triumphant close in F major.

Second movement: Andante (CD Track 2)

At the helm of this movement, which Brahms composed in advance of the others, is a poem by the German poet Sternau:

> The twilight falls, the moonlight gleams
> Two hearts in love unite
> Embraced in blissful rapture

No one should presume for a moment that the inclusion of this sentimental throwaway, a refugee from the age of landscape poetry, is an example of Brahms paying homage to program music. At least the quotation is mercifully short. While it may serve as an innocent metaphor for the mood, if not the substance or purpose, of the music itself, I see it as an instruction earmarked for the pianist, every bit as pragmatic, in its way, as a "poco crescendo" or "subito piano" marking.

Certainly, the poem's key words—*moonlight, twilight, love, embrace, blissful, rapture*—suggest an obvious translation, if you will, into the vocabulary of musical dynamics. Indeed, the poem itself, when interpreted as a kind of dynamic marking in its own right, is as much a translation as it is a plea for musical intimacy. Intimacy is the poem's calling card, as it is this splendid Andante's. Eric Le Van again weighs in with a provocative thought on the issue of intimacy here:

> Seldom has the image of romantic love been so poignantly evoked as in the music that follows these stanzas. Candid tenderness, episodes of effusive intensity never outweigh, however, the predominant atmosphere of moonlit intimacy. All is tinged throughout with crepuscular hues, in that contemplative region situated somewhere—to quote Edgar Allan Poe—"as those mere points of time where the confines of the waking world blend with those of the world of dreams."

The principal melody establishes at once the new key of A-flat major. It forms an eerily calm string of eighth-notes that descend in thirds for a full bar (0:01) before angling upward again a bar later (0:06). This concave figuration, set against an innocuous though likewise placid drift of descending sixteenth-notes, is the very picture of a private aside, even on its own, wholly musical terms. It has no rests, no accents, no punctuation, and above all, no dynamic markings other than *piano*. It is a figure entirely devoid of swells or overt statement, of drama and restlessness; it is instead a serene and thoughtful evocation of a private confidence. Unity—another key word in Sternau's poem—finds itself duplicated in compositional categories by means of the parallel motion that articulates the trajectory of each voice. The sixteenth-notes that form the left-hand part ought not be construed to be a single voice; on the contrary, the left hand is an example of *contrapuntal melody,* wherein what appears at first to be a single melodic strand in fact harbors two or more consecutive melodies. In this case, the first, third, fifth, and seventh sixteenth-notes in the left hand form one voice, while the other voice, out of phase, forms the other (0:00–1:00). The pianist must be careful to segregate as well as connect these alternating voices with exceptional discretion.

The wistful second theme, assigned to the treble register against the drone of double thirds in the alto voice and the unobtrusive counterpoint in contrary motion below, bespeaks its innocence, as if it had never encountered another key in its short life (1:01). Brahms spreads out the bass in extensive but still slow-moving arpeggios en route to the D-flat major middle section, a nod to classicism if ever there was one.

For the lay listener unfamiliar with Brahms's score, the tempo marking of this new section (2:34) is particularly revealing. He writes "Poco più lento" (a little bit slower) but then adds, in German, "Ausserst leise und zart" (easygoing and tender). He also changes the meter from 2/4 to 4/16, an alteration that does nothing to alter the tempo per se (the relative rates of the sixteenths are identical in each section), at the same time subtly modifying both phrasing and accentuation.

Whereas the opening proceeds in uninterrupted if irregular two-bar phrases, now Brahms writes in rather straightforward four-bar units articulated by slurs adroitly placed over two sixteenth-note couplets in each measure. The effect, when properly conveyed (and with a slight emphasis given to the third of each four bars), is enchanting, engendering as it does a confidential dialogue supported by a lone D-flat pedal point that rings out soulfully in the bass on the first beat of each measure. This may refer to a distant bell, or to the hushed interjection of a far-off drum. In any case, the couplets form a lilting duet that contextually legitimizes their docile ebb and flow. The emphatic pedal point on D-flat, however, is sufficiently enlarged in the subsequent section (3:51), where Brahms again changes the metrical organization. Moving into 3/8 time, or three beats per bar, the accompanying bass evolves into a restless continuity of D-flats in the alto, tenor, and bass registers, colored only by a neighboring E-flat. The dynamic grows to a full *forte*, as the bass orbits around its D-flat pedal point (4:59). The upper voices proceed in sixths and widely arpeggiated chords, as they give shape to an extended melodic variant of the earlier couplets. Thus does Brahms transform, with uncommon urbanity, the quiet and imperturbable duet into something unusually rich and expressive.

Both the foregoing sections are repeated before the reestablishment of the principal theme, which restores the original meter of 2/4 (5:41). On this occasion, Brahms expands the role of the left hand, however, invigorating it as a configuration of triplets and considerably wider arpeggiations. The mood grows more anxious and impassioned, that is, until the reappearance of the first subordinate theme of the opening.

As the coda, marked "Andante molto," begins (marking a return, too, to D-flat major), Brahms is careful to provide instructions for pedaling (8:05). Though not as explicit as they might have been, these oblige the interpreter to use both the una corda (left pedal) and the damper (right pedal) simultaneously or in tandem. The consequent effect of such judicious pedaling, if carried out correctly, is to partially mute the strings of the piano at the same time it prolongs and gives echo to the piano's plentiful sonorities. The imposition here of a long and droning pedal point on A-flat in the bass again suggests off-stage timpani.

Floating atop this pedal point, which goes on for a full fourteen bars before alighting temporarily on a B-flat and A-natural, is an entirely new, if derivative, theme. The calm is preserved within the context of a triple piano, a dynamic level so quiet as to hear a pin drop. This new motivic material expands soon enough into an ecstatic and impassioned outcry (9:48), reaching its apex in a fortissimo mass of dominant-quality chords on the fifth degree of the dominant (10:14). Then, breathing its last, its grandeur exhausted, the coda drifts in diminuendo for only three bars, segueing into a chorale-like Adagio of quiet and majestic chords that bid the movement farewell (10:37). Following a brief reflection of the placid opening theme (11:20) is a final exhalation of widely spread arpeggiated chords, which roll downward to the work's blissful conclusion.

Third movement: Scherzo; Allegro energico

The swooshing diminished arpeggio that bushwhacks its way toward a high D-flat at the opening of this raucous scherzo is only the first of its many audacious elements. What Brahms could not quite bring himself to write in his symphonies—a more or less conventional scherzo that paid homage to Beethoven—he gives us here. Returning to the sonata's principal key, F minor, Brahms has already set this scherzo in a league of its own, in that humor, the form's sine qua non, is set aside in favor of a mood more serious, and even sinister.

The first, or A, section, is vivid enough. Indeed, with its jumpy, disjointed parade of dotted rhythms in octaves that land squarely every four bars on an accented chord, there is something Mephistophelean about its pugnacious profusions, suggesting the fraternal rowdiness of a German beer hall during Oktoberfest. Some seventeen bars into the work, a second theme, lean and determined as it makes its ascent in minor thirds, sprouts up quietly. The dynamic is *piano,* but the mood is no less mischievous. The accompanying bass echoes the dotted rhythm of the opening but is also distantly related in design to the dotted motive that inaugurates the Allegro maestoso.

In stark contrast, the ensuing B section pursues a new motive, a ghostly arpeggiated figure that spans all of five notes descending from a high B-flat to the same note two octaves below. Like Wotan in Valhalla playing with his all-too-human subjects below without their knowledge, Brahms toys with this relentless motivic whisper for twenty-nine bars; it might be construed as a parody of the romantic opening bars of the Andante. At the same time the accompanying bass creeps forward with ascending octaves that skip one to the other in minor and major thirds.

A reprise of the A section concludes with a cascade of octaves and heavily accented downbeats and chords. Embracing convention at last, Brahms then introduces a trio in D-flat major, a key perfectly suited for its woodsy evocation of French horns and nature. There is nothing in the least sardonic or jittery here, but quite the opposite. Save for a few foreboding bars where four repeated notes (a reference at once to the second theme of the first movement, and deliberately or not to the celebrated fate motive that launches Beethoven's Fifth) hum menacingly as they migrate briefly to E-flat minor, the ambience is one of utter calm and serenity.

With the trio's conclusion, the A section returns and the scherzo comes to its uncompromising close on two weighty F minor chords.

Fourth movement: Intermezzo (Rückblick); Andante molto

That Brahms chose to include an intermezzo in such a large-scale work is perhaps not so much the stuff of musical innovation as of musical strategy. Indeed, just in case anyone should forget, Brahms carefully attaches the word "Rückblick" (in retrospect). And that is precisely what this movement is: a reminiscence that encapsulates the principal motivic ideas, but also the moods, of the entire sonata thus far. If there is one thing that stands out as most significant about this movement, it is that it avoids looking forward; there is not a single reference to any of the themes set forth in the Finale. That constitutes, in its own way, a kind of existential angst, especially in light of the somewhat cinematic character of this Intermezzo: while summing up its parts, it also accounts for their absence.

Here Brahms moves to B-flat minor and combines two motives familiar from the previous three movements: first, a variant of the four-note repeated motive that informs the second theme of the Allegro maestoso and that raised its defiant head, too, in the trio of the Scherzo; and a variant of the placid eight-note descending motive that defines the principal material of the slow movement Andante. As Eric Le Van points out, here it becomes "a tragic and almost bitter metamorphosis of the blissful Andante theme. It is an emblem of love gone awry, as if to say that happiness never lasts; the loss is irremediable."

The relentless reiteration of the four-note motive—Brahms's reinvention of the celebrated fate motive from Beethoven's Fifth—informs the funereal character of this movement, the shortest of the five. A brief respite from the sepulchral overtones, some nineteen bars into the Intermezzo, gives way to an ethereal array of perfect and diminished fifths distributed between the hands in contrary motion. The mood resumes its grim countenance only a few bars later as the "fate" motive, now fortissimo and further exacerbated by an accelerando, focuses laserlike on accentuated rootless chords that climb upward from the bass in a terrifying fanfare. No matter how much he may have disdained the idea of extramusical meaning, Brahms would himself have been hard-pressed to deny that these trumpetlike heralds bring a vision of death. The Intermezzo fades away in pianissimo, the fate motive, now punctuated by rests, resigned to its own destiny.

Fifth movement: Finale; Allegro moderato ma rubato (CD Track 3)

The foregoing four movements of this magniloquent sonata are a tough act to follow. But that hardly fazed the young Johannes Brahms. Here, he lavishes his compositional gifts on a rondo, with elements of a tarantella. The gruff but oddly playful material that forms the opening theme presents its case in the lower registers in imitation of the cellos and basses in the orchestrated version that this work could so easily have become. The rhythmic impetus drives along in eighth-notes, its dotted rhythms infused with their composer's love of all things Italian.

As the work ascends into a higher register, Brahms intensifies the activity with an instruction to play "più agitato"—with greater excitement—only to be followed a few bars later with the instruction "molto agitato" (0:28 and 0:36). The dynamic, now *fortissimo,* favors the onslaught of sixteenths in counterpoint with a variant of the opening theme rushing upward in the bass.

A change of key signature (to one flat) heralds a broad and impassioned second theme emerging in F major, accompanied by a restless rustle of sixteenths in the bass and tenor voices (0:54). In professional music circles, as we have seen, the first three of these notes, F, A, and E, have become the subject of a well-known anecdote, in that they correspond to the dictum *Frei aber einsam* (Free but lonely), attributed to Joseph Joachim. Four flats reappear in the key signature, but this time they denote A-flat major, rather than F minor, as the home key. A pastiche of arpeggiated chords breezes along blithely above a particularly insistent pedal point on a single D-flat in the bass en route to a reprise of the original theme (2:02).

Chorales became elements of Brahms's compositional vocabulary in the symphonies. But here Brahms provides a preview of what is to come in one of his noblest. A weighty chorale in D-flat major surfaces as the movement's third subject, fleshing out this rondo with compassion and nobility. Its cantus firmus (a melody that serves as the fundament for polyphonic development) is significant for the role it assumes for the remainder of the movement (3:26).

Indeed, as tension mounts and the tempo accelerates, the tonality again migrates to F major. The cantus firmus of the chorale is recycled and celebrated in diminution. It is offered up first in the left hand alone, under the tempo marking "più mosso," as if it is destined to become the subject of a fugue (6:23). But Brahms surprises us by reinventing it as the first salvo in an orgy of polyphony. Surprisingly, the texture of the passage is relatively thin, at least for a while, highlighting its admittedly consistent metrical organization of six eighth-notes per bar with unusual vivacity. Into this frenzy the left hand reintroduces the now familiar opening motive of the movement, which scampers to and fro in double thirds (6:41). Accelerating to a whirlwind presto wherein virtually every register of the piano is vibrantly exploited, the sonata exhausts itself in an ecstatic, even delirious coda (6:55). A triumphant chordal conclusion, imaginary trumpets and trombones ablaze (7:33), brings the sonata to its heroic close.

Klavierstücken (Piano Pieces)

To throw the thirty-four individual works that constitutes the seven opuses of Brahms's Klavierstücken into the general category of "miniatures" strikes me as gross understatement. For one thing, the term itself has a pejorative side and risks being misunderstood, especially among those who may be entirely unfamiliar with the music. There is nothing either superficial or particularly entertaining about this collection of intermezzos, rhapsodies, capriccios, romances, and ballades. On the contrary, these are without exception thoughtful, introspective, and pristinely constructed compositions, which, in light of their overall substance and breadth, merit substantive critical appreciation and informed interpretation.

Thus let us briefly survey a representative swath of these works, whose composition extends from Brahms's youth to old age, with a view toward grasping whatever we can of their essence. Here we will examine all four of the "King Edward" Ballades, as well as works from Opuses 76, 79, 117, and 118. In spite of their abbreviated forms, these masterpieces are complex and their beauties innumerable. Indeed, they reflect precisely what Brahms invested in them: the breadth of his experience and imagination, and the technical and aesthetic resources that he put at the disposal of his overwhelming ingenuity and genius.

Four Ballades, Op. 10 ("King Edward")

No. 1 in D minor: Andante; Allegro ma non troppo
No. 2 in D major: Andante; Allegro non troppo
No. 3 in B minor: Allegro (CD Track 4)
No. 4 in B major: Andante con moto; Più lento (CD Track 5)

No matter how often he changed his mind, threw away scores, rearranged his compositions, or refused commissions, Brahms was hardly flippant. Certainly, 1854 proved a remarkable year for him. Not only did his idol, Robert Schumann, welcome him as a protégé, but it was also the year that saw the maturation of his compositional gifts. Indeed, between 1852 and 1854 he composed several of his finest and most celebrated works, including his three magniloquent piano sonatas, the Piano Trio Op. 1, the Variations on a Theme by Schumann, and the four "King Edward" Ballades, Op. 10.

Julius O. Grimm should certainly have been thrilled to learn that his friend Brahms had dedicated the Ballades to him, yet given the inspiration for the set, one can only wonder if Herr Grimm felt any sting in being named the object of Brahms's compositional affection. After all, Brahms drew inspiration for these concise but masterful works from an ancient Scottish ballad, Edward, a story of patricide. Brahms was familiar with the poem in the German translation by the poet and philosopher Johann Gottfried Herder (1744–1803):

> Why does your sword so drip with blood, Edward, Edward?
> And why so sad are ye?
> "Oh, I have killed my hawk so fine . . ."

The Ballades Op. 10 must have sounded very peculiar to Brahms's contemporaries. In an era that favored virtuosity, empty display, and the sensuous pleasures of a pianistic bel canto, these ballades, sparse and severe, promised just the opposite. Brahms eschewed precisely what Liszt embraced at that time. (Though they remained for years in opposition to each other's artistic viewpoint, Liszt eventually came to appreciate and even share something of Brahms's aesthetic philosophy, abandoning the vocabulary of virtuosity in favor of an exceptionally lean but immensely expressive compositional style not at all far removed from these Ballades.)

The first ballade, a simple ternary form in D minor, mirrors the uneasy consternation of the poem. A grim procession of widely spaced chords glides by quietly in quarter-note motion. The open fifths in their bass register, looking back to a much earlier era of musical composition, inform their presence as something at once unsettling and timeless. As the tempo accelerates slightly from "andante" to "poco più moto," the harmonic rhythm also moves more quickly. Here, Brahms anticipates a compositional vocabulary he would cultivate later in life with incomparable finesse. The subtle coloration of the prevailing harmony with hints of foreign tonalities alienates stability and leaves us yearning for resolution that is subsequently denied. The heroic middle section amplifies both tempo and texture as the key shifts to D major. But the mood, though brighter, is not so much optimistic as it is grimly determined. Brahms again appropriates a motivic figure that he would continue to employ all his life: the four-note "fate" motive that opens Beethoven's Fifth Symphony. As the dynamic enlarges to *fortissimo,* the thematic material of the first section returns, but in reverse; the eerie opening chords take a second position, the bass now modified to offer itself as a gentle sequence of ambulatory, truncated triplets that proceed in staccato eighth-notes. The work comes to a dark close as the bass elaborates its foregoing material, coming to rest on a hushed D minor chord.

Two bars of a D major triad, configured in octaves alongside a bass accompaniment of syncopated pulsations, form the brief introduction to the A section of the second ballade. From this blossoms a theme at once veiled and comforting that, in its gentle descent, echoes the principal melody of the F Minor Piano Sonata's Andante. Here, too, Brahms evokes time and distance by means of intervallic space, its abundant melodic progression of thirds and sixths played astride the stream of single, off-beat eighths below. The vigorous Allegro non troppo that follows introduces the B section in B minor with a defiant new theme. Bold accents modify a steady sequence of four repeated eighths, which continually expand outward into octaves, and thick, secondary dominant chords. Emerging on its heels is a swift and elusive variant of the principal theme, its texture thinned as it is now configured, in B major, as an unwieldy array of triplets, each note of which is modified by an appoggiatura from below. Marked "Molto staccato e leggiero," its stream of notes whispers along like a chill wind until the return of the B section twenty-one bars later. The return of the A section is distinguished by a placid coda that combines, in the tenor and bass, the material configuration of the work's two-bar introduction along with a fragment of the principal theme.

Unsettling, jagged, and mercurial syncopated rhythms define the outer sections of the third ballade (CD Track 4). In B minor and marked "Allegro," it opens ambiguously with three heavily accented open fifths in the bass, each configured as an upbeat (0:00). But they do not behave at all like upbeats; on the contrary, disguised as down-beats, they confound expectation. On their heels, the principal theme is a mischievous sequence of truncated motivic fragments (0:03). Each motivic cell comprises a dotted eighth-note that forms a dissonance with an arpeggiated flurry of three sixteenths, which grow out of it and are then cut short by an accented eighth-note. Separating each of these motivic fragments is an eighth-rest adroitly placed on the weak fifth beat of each bar. The tension is palpable as a spirited second theme, in syncopated chords and octaves, saunters forward in contrary motion (0:11). An ethereal B section in F-sharp major proceeds with celestial airiness in the piano's upper registers as a chain of falling perfect fourths and fifths gently caresses the stream of *pianissimo* chords that float above it (1:51). The music's mood is consistent with its sister ballades', in that timelessness and memory are again evoked through registrational distance, open fifths, rootless harmonies, and quiescent dynamics in which the harmonies seem to materialize gradually, as if from off stage. The last twelve bars of this section give emphasis to these features, as they engage a haunting dialogue in thirds juxtaposed over distant registers (2:45). This lilting interplay of thirds tossed between the stratospheric region of the treble and the sultry domain of the alto rock gently over a double pedal point on F-sharp and a lightly accented A-sharp above it.

The A section discreetly reinstates itself in B minor (3:01), casting its capricious motivic figure in pianissimo as it shifts into B major one last time (3:27). Things come to a tranquil rest on a subdued mediant chord (that is, a chord built upon the third degree of the scale—3:38), which in turn morphs almost imperceptibly into a conclusive, *pianississimo* B major triad.

The appealing lyricism of the fourth and final ballade (CD Track 5) is well suited to the extended four-bar phrases that enliven it. It evolves from the quiescent concluding bars of the previous movement by virtue of its key, B major. But here Brahms proffers a broad and efflorescent melody so endearing as to suggest that he might have conceived it as a song, rather than a piano piece. Indeed, like a human voice, the melody floats blithely in four-bar phrases over a lightly descending arpeggio (0:00–0:08). Dividing the A section into two parts, Brahms maintains throughout both the structure and integrity of each voice, finally coming to cadence on the tonic B some forty-six bars into the piece.

What follows, in the dominant F-sharp major, is an extraordinary bit of polyphonic writing, a hush of triplets over duplets below (1:47). Brahms's instructions couldn't be more specific: "Più lento, con intimissimo sentimento ma senza troppo marcare la Melodia" (A bit slower, with intimate sentiment, but without undue emphasis of the melody). That is particularly well put, because embedded within these hypnotic undulations are two discreetly ambulant voices, in the alto and tenor, that move ineluctably forward over a persistent, if not omnipresent, tonic pedal. The return of the A section, which restores the ballade to its home key of B major, is remarkable for its playfulness and eloquence (4:37). The accompanying descent in eighth-notes, now lightly inflected in staccato, is also modified by the periodic infusion of two sixteenths per bar.

What ensues is an entirely new section, unexpected in that it disrupts the ternary form we had come to expect; its thematic design is a variant of the principal melody (5:05). It is a reverent, comforting, and dignified chorale that seems to speak not only on behalf of this particular ballade, but also for the entire set; indeed, its meandering harmonic progression, awash in the colors of secondary dominants and wholly alien tonalities, boasts a certain wanderlust. The final page delicately elaborates the polyphonic strands of the B section, expanding them slightly with octave doublings and hairpin crescendos (7:09). In the penultimate bar (8:15), the triplets and duplets in tandem swell and diminish, drawing this intimate ballade to a fundamentally optimistic conclusion.

Capriccio Op. 76, No. 5
Agitato, ma non troppo presto (*Sehr aufgeregt, doch nicht so schnell*)

This sultry, dark-hued work, composed in 1878, belongs to a set of eight works comprising four capriccios and four intermezzos. While a capriccio cannot aspire to the rigorous formal constraints, or even traditions, of sonata form, it is nevertheless a compositional genre that stretches back centuries.

On the whole, the capriccio has long been music's favorite bad boy. Usually a short, rhapsodic, and free-spirited work that challenges convention and favors sharp contrasts, the capriccio is well known for sporting brilliant and often bizarre figurations, asymmetrical rhythms, and a rhapsodic air that sets it apart from any other genre. It gained popularity long before the birth of Brahms, having been elaborated and put to use just as frequently in the Renaissance and baroque eras as it was in the nineteenth century. Indeed, it was a favorite of early Italian keyboard composers, including Frescobaldi and Vivaldi.

Brahms was fond of all things Italian and vacationed in Italy in his later years. Though he had no particular interest in assimilating Italian musical traditions, as Chopin did, into his own compositional style, the fact remains he was an authority on early choral and keyboard music. It is unlikely that the capriccio, and the rich potential it promised, could have escaped his attention. Given his lifelong love for and fascination with Gypsy music, too, with its minefield of cross-rhythms, hemiolas, and odd accentuations—compositional devices ideally suited for fulfilling the ethos of a capriccio—it is no wonder he developed affection for it.

The Capriccio in C-sharp Minor, while hardly formless, evokes something of the strange and rhapsodic character that gave the genre its reputation. Though the time signature specifies 6/8 (that is, six beats to a bar), this capriccio aspires to difference. This work is an exercise in cross-rhythms, creating crosscurrents in simultaneous duple and triple meters. It opens with three distinct themes (or "voices," as musicians call them), though the lowest one is doubled in octaves. The principal theme, an ominous ascending motive in quarter notes—three to the bar—presides in the soprano voice as it proceeds cautiously in stepwise motion. The tenor voice underneath likewise oscillates and stretches upward, but at double the pace as it slithers forward in six eighths per bar. Punctuating this polyphonic frenzy is the bass, which assumes a deliberate stride as it straddles only two beats per bar, each beat coinciding on the first and fourth eighth-note above it. However, this is not an example of Brahms's favorite two-against-three rhythm, wherein the second note of a duplet falls quite literally in between the second and third notes of a triplet. Instead, the metrical organization is such that each voice aspires to autonomy as it moves forward within its own temporal sphere.

The texture thickens some nineteen bars into the piece, giving way to a new motivic fragment. Here another voice emerges and the key migrates briefly, though not definitively, to E major and B major. The shift of tonality is transitional; it is a coloration more than a formal modulation. The pace picks up, too, as a flurry of sixteenths in the alto voice agitates the density and moves things along in a steady stream of syncopes and hemiolas in octaves. Following the return of the principal thematic material, the tempo relaxes a bit under Brahms's instructive "poco tranquillo." Here, an expressive inversion of the opening theme, now tender and elegiac, drifts downward in the soprano, but more than an octave higher than its position at the beginning of the work. The middle section offers a mini-development of the thematic material, first elaborating the syncopes and hemiola rhythm that formed the second thematic group, and then treating the principal theme to diminution, that is, condensing its rhythmic organization. What had started out as three quarter-beats per bar at the work's outset now materializes as a vigorous tumble of eight sixteenth-notes per bar. But the rhythm soon expands again, as the principal theme mutates into a passionate tug of ascending octaves articulated in slurred eighth-notes atop a compressed variant of the same motive, configured in sixteenths, in the tenor voice below.

Like a powerful ocean tide, the thematic material pulls itself upward in small dynamic waves, reaching an impassioned climax that restores both breadth and temporal value to the melodic fragments. A pulsating pedal point on G-sharp in the bass serves to prolong the tension before the texture thins out and fades to a whisper. The ensuing coda restores but also varies the multiple meters of the opening, expanding from a hushed whisper to a crashing *fortissimo* in a mere seven bars. Here the bass, which now declines to proceed in two beats per bar, pummels downward in consecutive phrase units of five eighth-notes, displacing strong beats and disrupting the metrical organization. The capriccio concludes with three blustery chords that move from dominant to tonic, evidence enough that Brahms was not one to ignore convention.

Intermezzo Op. 76, No. 3, in A-flat Major
Grazioso; Anmutig, ausdrucksvoll

Unlike the capriccio, the intermezzo has its genesis in theater. In the late baroque and early classical eras, its name referred to an *entr'acte,* that is, a comedic work inserted between the acts of an opera. Perhaps it is no accident that Brahms again looks toward Italian conventions without appropriating either the style or techniques that inform them. In any case, by the nineteenth century, the intermezzo assumed a rather different meaning, purpose, and form that had little if anything to do with opera. Instead, it came to be construed as a short, whimsical work that, like its theatrical ancestor, could be positioned within a larger work or survive independently as a so-called character piece.

The Intermezzo Op. 76, No. 3, is a little bit of both. Though it is certainly an autonomous confection that stands quite on its own alongside other such pieces collected in a single opus, it is not, strictly speaking, a movement in a suite. Brahms was just as happy to have these works played singly as he was to hear them all performed consecutively. Indeed, in this and his other late opuses, there is no continuous or overriding thematic thread that links one work structurally to another, though one can certainly argue the presence of a common ambience or mood. (The first two of the Three Intermezzi, Op. 117, might be an exception, as both are inspired by a single poem and codify, to a certain extent but not rigidly, its strophic organization.) That commonality is likely a consequence of Brahms's compositional process, and the fact that he composed each of these works, save for the first of the set, at the same time. (The opening Capriccio, Op. 76, No. 1, in F-sharp Major, is an exception; it was composed seven years earlier.)

The delicate, crystalline figure that launches this elegant capriccio does so atop a persistent pedal point on the tonic A-flat below. The entrance of the principal theme, a graceful, descending chain of sixths and thirds in the upper registers of the piano, is delayed by the placement of an eighth-rest, instead of a note, on the very first beat. The resulting displacement of the metrical foot has the effect of shifting the melody slightly forward and ahead of the left hand, which proceeds more or less conventionally in a steady stream of eighth-notes.

Of particular interest are the arpeggiations Brahms specifically indicates in the lower voices, and this compels me to digress for a moment. While this device lends considerable charm to the music, reinforces the aforementioned pedal point, and clarifies harmonic rhythm, it also brings up another issue, perhaps not so often discussed, and that is performance practice—and the view that Brahms may have taken of it. That he inserted these arpeggios suggests it may have been a dim one. It was not uncommon in the nineteenth century for pianists to roll chords, adding arpeggiations here and there and playing the right hand (or whatever hand carried the principal melody at a given time) a wee bit ahead of or behind the left. Some pianists tended to exaggerate this practice, thus throwing things totally out of proportion and distorting both the letter and spirit of the music. Even today, students, enamored of the so-called "golden age" of pianism, indulge in such practices as a means to prove how "artistic" they are, or to show off what they know of the performance practices of a century ago.

Of course, that such misinformed ideas proceed from a gross misunderstanding of both the purpose and extent of such practices doesn't bother the piano prima donnas in the least. Even so, I have to wonder if Brahms, who not only was a stickler for accuracy, but favored performers who respected his compositional intentions, had something else in mind when writing this intermezzo. Though my thoughts here are purely speculative, it is as if he didn't want to leave it to chance that a performer, in a fit of indulgence, would be able to resist the temptation to arpeggiate a little too often.

Whatever the case, the musical temperature increases as an expressive new section, availing itself of an authentic two-against-three rhythm, proceeds in light, dominant-quality chords. The lilting syncopes here continue to a velvety climax that, interpreted contextually (and in light of the overall dynamic markings), culminates in *pianissimo*. It's an exquisite moment that demands a pianist of exceptional finesse and sensitivity. Following the return of the principal thematic material, the intermezzo again darkens as the theme lumbers to the lower registers, all the while slackening its pace in its metrical shift to 3/2 time, and concludes much as it began: with subdued and quiet dignity.

Rhapsody in G Minor, Op. 79, No. 2 (CD Track 6)
Molto passionato, ma non troppo allegro

No one will deny that this is the most famous of Brahms's three rhapsodies for piano. In his hands, it is not quite so freewheeling a form as some might believe. The rhapsodies of Brahms have little in common with Liszt's Hungarian Rhapsodies, for example, in spite of the interest both had in Hungarian folk music and the subsequent influence that Magyar culture exerted on them both. But Brahms's rhapsodies are neither episodic nor virtuosic; neither feverish pyrotechnics nor exaggerated sentiments inform them.

On the contrary, the Brahms G Minor Rhapsody, like its sister, Op. 79, No. 1, in B Minor, is a model of classical sonata form. The use of this form hardly diminishes the fundamental spirit, signified by the title, of either work. The very first thing Brahms indicates alongside the tempo marking is "molto passionato," suggesting that he was determined, especially in such a compact form, to codify and convey an emotional state.

This rhapsody, like so much of Brahms's piano music, is conceptually an orchestral work. Its famous opening theme bellows forth in the upper voice, set firmly in the middle range of the piano, in ascending thirds (0:00). Its three-part texture stays afloat over a continuous triplet accompaniment in the middle voice, while weighty octaves define the bass. Although the pianist, who must cross left hand over right in order to play the melody (at least as it is notated, with slurs of the second and third beats of the bar), is largely responsible for maintaining the prevailing legato, the very sight of these frequent hand crossings, for the concertgoer, adds something to the overall mood of earnest consternation. The second subject is a bold, even militaristic parade of fat chords and jumpy octaves, which leap about in the left hand like an escaped fugitive mouthing in the shadows (0:21).

Brahms was never at a loss for melody. He harvested as much thematic material as he could for inclusion in his expositions, elaborating melodic ideas by means of variation and imitation. Doing as much here, he introduces an exotic new theme in contrast to the bellicose chordal procession that precedes it. It is a melody that bears the unmistakable air of a Gypsy violin, its undulating chromaticism conveying, too, something of the slithering elisions and oily glissandi that are the anthem of seduction (0:34).

The third phase of the exposition is the stuff of toil and trouble; it is a march that exploits the lower register in menacing octaves in quarter-notes and an uneasy dotted rhythm (0:53). As he so often does, Brahms, like the devil, mixes truth with lies, at least metaphorically speaking: he gambles with major and minor tonalities, intertwining them as a means of creating both compositional ambiguity and, in the household of perception, emotional anxiety. The music heaves and hoes, elaborating its three themes before reestablishing them in the recapitulation. The now-familiar dotted motive in octaves expands into dominance in the coda, which rises to a blistering *fortissimo* (6:07). Just as swiftly, the texture thins out in a slow, written-out trill that fades away into *pianissimo,* only to be forcefully and unexpectedly contradicted by two huge *fortissimo* chords, dominant to tonic, bringing this most unrhapsodic of rhapsodies to its heroic end.

Intermezzo Op. 117, No. 2 (CD Track 7)
Andante non troppo e con molta espressione

This brooding intermezzo raises more questions than it answers, and one question in particular strikes me as worthy of discussion. Thus, before moving on to an analysis of this brief but haunting work, let's take a deeper look at an enigma that is as much concerned with the life of Johannes Brahms as it is implicitly connected to this particular piece.

By 1892, the bachelor Brahms, whose history with women was awash in neurosis, had long since given up any hope of entering into a romantic relationship with Clara Schumann, much less marrying her. Doubtless heartbroken by Clara's failure to requite his affections in the way he would have liked, he met Agathe von Siebold, whom he came close to marrying. His intentions were certainly serious; he even immortalized her name through musical codification, making the notes A–G–A–H–E the thematic basis for the second subject of the first movement of his G Major Sextet, Op. 36. But after a chilly warning from Clara, who took a dim view of this potential union, he changed his mind, abandoning the poor girl to her own devices. He took a liking to Julie Schumann, Clara's daughter, expressing his frustration upon hearing that she had married an Italian count. Later in life he developed a crush on Hermine Spies, whom he met in the countryside while on holiday and who, like all the other women he admired romantically (save for Clara), was a singer. But when winter rolled around they parted company, and again Brahms's interest cooled as quickly as water at zero degrees. When his feelings became a bit too overheated with his piano student Elisabeth von Stockhausen, with whom he remained friendly even after she married the composer Heinrich von Herzogenberg, he again took flight. Finally, there was Alice Barbi, a rather large lady fond of ample furs and big hats, whom he befriended in Vienna in the 1890s and who, for all intents and purposes, became his last paramour.

And what does all this have to do with an intermezzo that lasts barely four minutes? Well, quite possibly nothing at all. But then again, the poem that inspired this work is "Lady Anne Bothwell's Lament," an Elizabethan-era ballad of anonymous authorship that turned up in a collection of such works discovered and assembled by Bishop Thomas Percy in 1765. As we shall see, it may well have inspired Brahms, the tireless allusionist, for other, rather extramusical reasons that, to my knowledge, no one to date has bothered to investigate.

As for the poem itself, it concerns a heartbroken woman, Lady Anne Bothwell, who, abandoned by her lover, has given birth to his son. Bemoaning her fate and addressing her child, she reveals her sordid past and expresses her regret, not for her actions, but for her naiveté. In a burst of Elizabethan machismo, her lover, it seems, has gone off to war. She beseeches her boy to honor his father nevertheless, because only God is fit to judge the actions of a cad.

The poem itself is unusually expressive, even musical, and in light of what it might really have meant to Brahms, the following excerpted stanzas (four out of thirteen) merit our attention, if not scrutiny:

Ballad XXVIII
Lady Anne Bothwell's Lament

Balow, my boy, ly still and sleep,
It grieves me sore to hear thee weep,
If thou'lt be silent, I'll be glad,
Thy mourning makes my heart full sad.
Balow, my boy, thy mother's joy,
Thy father bred one great annoy.
Balow, my boy, ly still and sleep,
It grieves me sore to hear thee weep.

When he began to court my love,
And with his sugar'd words to move,
His tempting face, and flatt'ring chear,
In time to me did not appear;
But now I see that cruel he
Cares neither for his babe nor me.

Balow, my boy, thy father's fled,
When he the thriftless son has played;
Of vows and oaths forgetful, he
Preferr'd the wars to thee and me.
But now, perhaps, thy curse and mine
Make him eat acorns with the swine.

Balow, my boy, I'll weep for thee;
Too soon, alake, thou'lt weep for me:
Thy griefs are growing to a sum,
God grant thee patience when they come;
Born to sustain thy mother's shame,
A hapless fate, a bastard's name.
Balow, my boy, ly still and sleep,
It grieves me sore to hear thee weep.

Brahms cites only the opening couplet atop the first page of the first intermezzo in this opus (Op. 117, No. 1), in a translation by the German poet and philosopher Johann Gottfried Herder. It may be significant for what it doesn't say as much as for what it does. Indeed,

Brahms referred to these melancholy intermezzi as "three lullabies to my sorrows." But why?

A well-known myth holds that the teenage Brahms, in an effort to support himself and his family, worked in brothels, playing popular music as the libidinous clientele went about their business. Most scholars have disputed that legend and conclusively proven it to be either hearsay or fanciful invention of his early biographers. The fact is that Brahms did work as a pianist in local Hamburg taverns, where prostitutes and every manner of ne'er-do-well lurked.

In his paper "Brahms, Solitary Altruist" (*Brahms and His World*, Princeton University Press, 1990), psychiatrist Peter F. Ostwald, whose psychoanalytic biography of Robert Schumann revealed much uncomfortable information about that great composer's compulsive disorders, ventures a provocative opinion:

> Sexuality clearly seems to have been a problem for Brahms. He was able to be affectionate with women, even demonstrative at times (as suggested by photographs, although these are mostly of the older Brahms and tend to show the women hugging him rather than vice versa). His habitual caution if not abhorrence in regard to physical intimacy may reflect traumatic childhood experiences, with parents who were unhappily married, often at cross-purposes, and perhaps abusive at times. His reserve toward women may also have been conditioned by the climate of sexual promiscuity in the Hamburg taverns where he had worked a teenager. Hitschmann described it this way: "Too early he came to know the active, frivolous, purchasable sexuality of the prostitute. He once told of scenes he had witnessed: of the sailors who rushed into the inn after a long voyage, greedy for drinks, gambling, and love of women, who, half-naked, sang their obscene songs to his accompaniment, then took him on their laps and enjoyed awakening his first sexual feelings." (Hitschmann citation from *Great Men,* p. 212)

Whether the last "who" in Hitschmann's statement ("*who,* half-naked, sang their obscene songs") refers to the sailors or to the women is unclear. Certainly the structure of the sentence and the position of its dependent clauses suggest the latter. In any case, the idea that Brahms favored engaging prostitutes now and then has met with little resistance among scholars. Given his circumstances as a single man whose issues with intimacy sometimes compelled him to abandon the women he loved, it is hardly an unreasonable assumption.

Of all the poems he might have chosen, given his penchant for cryptic reference and, as we have seen, for musical allusion, why did he select this one? By 1892, Brahms had already announced his retirement. Only two years earlier he had written his publisher Simrock, saying, "With this note you can take leave of my music, because it is high time to stop." Of course, he did not, though he slowed down a bit, and Op. 117 is only one of the fruits of his last years. Though there is no telling if he had any foreboding or sense of the illness that would end his life only five years later, he seemed to intuit that his career was winding down. As always anxious about his legacy and how his life's work would be judged and interpreted by posterity, he wrote to a number of his friends and acquaintances, including Clara Schumann, asking them to destroy his personal correspondence. Some did (including Clara, who at least had the good sense to hold on to some of it), though most didn't, with good reason.

That he asked them to do so offers no concrete evidence whatsoever about his sexual liaisons over the years, nor does it furnish even an iota of proof that he knowingly sired an illegitimate child. But it does support his reputation as an essentially secretive man who held his cards exceptionally close to his vest. He was no friend to loneliness, but he embraced solitude. This he did not out of misanthropy, but out of artistic necessity. He valued his private space and time as the best and most efficient means to accomplish his life's difficult work. His private life was his own business, and like most celebrities, he was not exactly keen on the idea of having it become public knowledge.

Of course, Brahms had an advantage that a man of his public stature would never be able enjoy today—to wit, a relatively limited media apparatus that, even at its most critical, more often than not overlooked the troubles of society's most prominent citizens and also respected their privacy. He was, after all, a wealthy man with a stellar reputation and, in spite of his sometimes gruff manners, widely admired for his generosity. If he did sire an illegitimate son or daughter, and knew of it, he was sufficiently well-heeled and connected to make the problem go away quietly and legally.

The relevant question, then, is not if or whether he did so, but if, in alluding to the Lady Anne Bothwell, he was trying to leave posterity a clue. Was the shrewd and image-conscious Brahms attempting, in some oddly personal way, to clear his conscience? Were these "lullabies to my sorrows" a repentant admission to a yet-unborn father confessor? Did his anxiety over his posthumous reputation extend to what his illegitimate progeny, if informed of their paternity, might say about him? Or did he simply want to leave behind, as most people do, some physical embodiment of his flesh and blood and, perhaps by proxy, his genius?

It is more likely that his selection of the Bothwell poem fulfilled another kind of regret, one born of fantasy. That Brahms had every opportunity to father children with any number of "respectable" mates, but chose not to, may well have inspired in him a rich fantasy life that allowed him to envision paternity as well as to mourn its absence.

Raising these questions may suggest an agenda, the intent of which is to indict, on the flimsiest of evidence, a cultural icon. On the other hand it is surprising that not one of Brahms's biographers has thoroughly investigated the possibility of his paternity. Certainly, even in the absence of proof, it is hardly unreasonable to presume that, in the course of some fifty years, even a man of Brahms's elevated stature might have unintentionally or unknowingly fathered a child. Notwithstanding his modesty and reputation for personal integrity in all his affairs, both personal and professional, the fact remains that no one knows with any degree of certainty just how many liaisons he may have enjoyed—that is, beyond his affairs with "respectable" women.

Indeed, there is one story that says a great deal about his character. Once, while on a stroll with one of his well-heeled society friends, Frau Bruell, he was embarrassed when a streetwalker shouted something at him. Whether she just recognized him as a local celebrity or was merely trying to draw attention to her buxom figure is not as telling as his reaction. "I want you to know," he told Frau Bruell, "that I have never made a married woman or a Fräulein unhappy!"

Given the lack of evidence or even referential accounts from either Brahms himself or his contemporaries, I would have to concur that he never had a child, and if he did, he certainly had no knowledge of it. What's more, a copy of Herder's *Stimme der Völker Liedern,* the volume in which his translation of the Bothwell poem was published, had been in Brahms's personal library for more than thirty-five years when he penned the Intermezzi Op. 117, having purchased it in 1856. Last but not least, it is impossible to ignore the fact that another Scottish poem, taken from the same volume of Herder, inspired one of Brahms's earliest works, the Ballades Op. 10. That poem, "Edward," concerned the grislier subject of patricide; yet we know for certain that Brahms never touched a hair on his father's head. So much, then, for any species of artificial rationalization that would construe fact from fantasy, or even vice versa.

These facts indeed suggest that Brahms's appropriation of the poem for inclusion alongside his Intermezzi Op. 117 is hardly evidence of a long-forgotten affair that bore fruit, but merely the melancholy reflections of an artist in search of an aesthetic way to express regret. Brahms, who valued his privacy and independence, was well aware of his limits as a man; he knew that having a wife and family would only compromise the purpose of his life and that the formation of such bonds would be as unfair to him as it would be to those he loved. His selfishness, at least in this particular realm of human relations, was neither ill-advised nor capricious, but thoughtfully considered. If Brahms had any agenda at all, it was to sublimate his earthly desires in favor of artistic expression. Even so, and especially in light of his musical philosophy, there is little if any demonstrable correspondence of affect that links, in any substantive way, his music to his personal life and desires.

In *Brahms and the German Spirit* (Harvard University Press, 2004), a provocative and thoughtful critique of Brahms in the context of German culture, Daniel Beller-McKenna offers the following assessment, which may shed some light on such conjecture and Brahms's disposition:

> Romantic Sehnsucht from Brahms's youth had developed by this point into mature melancholy: these [the late Intermezzi of Opuses 116–119] are not the affected musings of the "Junge Kreisler" (the later ego Brahms created in his youth to concretize the

identification with E.T.A. Hoffmann's imaginary *Kapellmeister*), but rather the reflections of an older man. Such sentiment runs throughout the Intermezzi. Often it is symbolized by musical displacements: harmonies, motives, or gestures which fall outside their proper musical context, thereby suggesting something that is remembered but that can no longer fit comfortably in the context in which it originally occurred.... As lullabies connote childhood, one could reasonably conjecture that Brahms's comment...speaks to his thoughts of his own youth. Accordingly the distant object of the opening lullaby [Op. 117, No. 1] might be a personal past that Brahms views from his sixties in pastoral imagery.... Thus the feeling of reminiscence expressed in this piece might indeed reflect the act of returning to an old valued source and the memories it evoked.

In raising the issue of Brahms's potential paternity, I do so not simply because the Lady Bothwell poem invites it, but as a means to challenge the wholesale lack of interest in this question. The position taken by biographers and critics is one of deference and respect, and rightfully so; in so doing, they honor, like executors of a vast estate, Brahms's wish that only his work, not the quotidian exigencies of his private life, be made fodder for public scrutiny. In this way, scholarship honestly enlists itself in the service of dissolving myths and fantasy that might otherwise get in the way of a fair, authentic, and ultimately useful debate on the merits of his artistic legacy. However, to marginalize and dismiss such issues as unworthy of attention serves only to allow apocryphal myths to flourish unchecked.

With these admittedly extramusical dimensions in mind, pianists have their work cut out for them. Musical interpretation demands a lot. In the case of the Intermezzo Op. 117, No. 2, pianists are charged with conveying the prevailing mood of sadness and regret, which is at once palpable and discreet, codified as it is in a chain of slurred two-note couplets deftly intertwined within a stream of arpeggios (0:00–0:47). Proceeding quietly in an alternate array of descending and ascending half-steps, whole-steps, and perfect fourths, these intervals, so adroitly built into the texture, exemplify *contrapuntal melody*, which we examined earlier in connection with the Andante of the F minor piano sonata. Every note is a thirty-second-note, though the slurred couplets, which unfold in the soprano voice, are either prolonged within the overall rhythmic design or gently emphatic.

However, I would be remiss if I did not put to rest the presumptuous and absolutely apocryphal notion that this intermezzo comprises only three voices, as there are in fact four. The melody and sparsely punctuated bass constitute two, while two groups of thirty-second-notes, which Brahms so carefully articulates under slurs, are assigned to the alto and tenor voices, respectively. A more pragmatic overview, for those who might have an opportunity to watch a pianist play this work up close, would clearly show that each of these groups is entrusted alternately to the pianist's right hand and left hand.

Though the key is B-flat minor, the harmonic rhythm is relatively quick; Brahms's fascination with tonal ambiguity expresses itself here with dominant-quality harmonies, which oscillate consistently between major and minor. Only eight bars into the work, a prolonged cadence on a most unusual arpeggio, based on a hybrid subdominant chord, compels the harmonic rhythm to slow down and yield to its will (0:21). This compositional device compromises a listener's inherited expectations and evokes a sense of foreboding. Even so, the motivic configuration remains steadfast as it repeats and then elaborates the original motive.

Thus far, and throughout the piece, there is a profusion of chromatic activity, that is, movement from a given pitch to the note just next to it, be it above or below. Although these specific motivic cells, as we have seen, are built into the theme as couplets and inform it, they also occur even more frequently in the tenor voice. However, the essential identity of this intervallic relationship does not necessarily rely on proximity, either. Though Brahms configures these sighing half-step and whole-step cells within the melody proper, they also enjoy a hidden life embedded within the arpeggios, though not necessarily next to each other. Indeed, they are also dispersed implicitly across time and bar lines, begging the adept listener to trace their destiny en route to both lower and higher registers.

With the introduction of a more placid second subject in D-flat major (1:08), Brahms intensifies the chromaticism in the alto and tenor voices, the counterpoint now clearly delineated as sixteenth notes in contrary motion (1:23). The texture here thickens, too, amplified by the nearly imperceptible addition of a fifth voice that complements the soprano at the distance of a third. Reestablishing its primacy, a variant of the principal thematic material surfaces, only to be disturbed, first by a diaphanous web of ascending and descending arpeggios (2:19), and then an array of lightly syncopated seventh chords (2:28). These in turn dissolve *pianissimo* into a fragile filigree of descending broken chords (2:38).

Not to be forgotten, the principal melody again asserts itself, this time expanding dynamically to the first of only two *fortes* in the entire work (3:32). As the tension increases, an emboldened cascade of arpeggios, enriched by octaves and a dominant pedal point on F, hemorrhages effortlessly into the coda (3:49). Here, both thematic subjects combine in yet another ambiguous shift of tonality, its harmonic coloration suggestive of both B-flat major and B-flat minor.

Of special interest here, though, is the appearance of a six-note figure in the soprano voice (3:57). Though a variant of the prolonged cadential arpeggio in the first section, it is perhaps no accident that it recalls another theme of Brahms's youth, which we have already examined, and that is the principal melody of both the Andante and Intermezzo (Rückblick) of the F Minor Sonata, Op. 5. But here the theme becomes self-referential as it acquires poignant new meaning, embroidered as it is within the larger temporal context of retrospect and regret. Where the F Minor Sonata's Andante concerns itself with a specific vision of romantic idealism start here ("Two hearts in love unite / Embraced in blissful rapture"); and just as the symbolic meaning of the Rückblick is bitter disillusionment with the defeated expectations and naiveté of youth, so this Intermezzo, Op. 117, No. 2, embraces a lifetime of regrets, of love lost, and of hopes shattered. It embroiders a rich fabric of signifiers, in that it also consumes the meaning of Brahms's earlier works, not the least of which is the F Minor Piano Sonata, for all their exuberance and youthful presumptuousness.

Perhaps, then, when considered in the larger context of his life and work, and also in relation to the Elizabethan poem of woe that he cites, there may be more to this brief work than meets the eye. I cannot presume to plumb its underlying meaning, at least beyond its compositional structure, or to have discovered some long-lost secret of Johannes Brahms. But dedicated interpreters will at least want to contemplate these issues in an effort to discern the appropriate tone, mood, and ethos of this delicate piece, and to disclose the affective camaraderie it shares conceptually with secrecy. Indeed, this enigmatic intermezzo has a vibrant but discreet inner life all its own, one that Brahms has exquisitely codified in its subtle, complex, and interdependent polyphony. To be sure, despite its size, its complexity is such that it discloses itself anew with every hearing, whispering its secrets and hushed asides to anyone willing and able to listen. Yes, the Intermezzo Op. 117, No. 2, has its secrets, all right, and it asks only that we don't give them up easily.

Intermezzo Op. 118, No. 6 (CD Track 8)
Andante, largo e mesto

The ambiguous tonality of this sweeping miniature tone poem in E-flat minor does nothing to compromise its intimacy or contained passion. Like its sister works in these late opuses, it comes into its own in a relatively straightforward ternary form—ABA. Its form notwithstanding, this work is a rapturous affair that proceeds from a single motivic cell, a mysterious, oscillating whisper of sixteenth-notes in the soprano voice extending over four bars and comprising only three neighboring pitches: G-flat, E-flat, and F-natural. This hypnotic fragment, which echoes the Dies Irae of the traditional Requiem Mass, positions itself as a kind of motivic mantra whose continuous repetition is as obsessive as it is self-serving (0:00–0:08). Indeed, from the very outset it drones on stubbornly against an upward swell of diminished arpeggios that, falling under its magnetic appeal, rises Lazarus-like from the sepulchral shadows (0:09). Even as this eerie theme doubles itself in a sinewy progression of major and minor thirds, dovetailing its doppelgängers along the way, the arpeggios below blow around it like a cold wind over a grave. The resulting dissonances don't jar us so much as they draw our attention to suspension: the suspension of pitch material, the suspension of resolution, and, most significant, the suspension of time.

That Brahms's overriding concern here is death, at least in the household of musical symbolism, is self-evident, and not only in consequence of his wholesale appropriation of the Dies Irae. This intermezzo's solemnity owes its power to a species of stasis that favors the gradual and almost imperceptible evolution of an organism. Mussorgsky did much the same, availing himself of a similar compositional aesthetic, but not vocabulary, in his opera *Khovanshchina*.

Although this intermezzo appears to bear witness to mortality, its pungent dissonances awash in pain and its voice, at least in the two outer sections, condemned like a silent scream to the most ethereal *pianissimo,* there also lurks something life-affirming under its otherwise uneasy surface. It evokes Nietzsche's Eternal Recurrence and the cycle that is life and death. In appropriating the Dies Irae, Brahms seems to summon death, yet at the same time, in transforming it into something as lasting, expressive, and material as a work of art—that is, the intermezzo itself—he negates its evocation of mortality and straddles a metaphorical threshold between existence and annihilation. From this perspective, no matter what parallels analysis may yield, and no matter what homology is created in an effort to link the work's musical vocabulary and symbols to issues of inherited experience, to say that this intermezzo is all about death doesn't quite ring true.

Certainly, its middle section comes to life quite on its own, its parade of thickening chords and martial rhythms orbiting around one predominant pitch, the dominant B-flat (2:00). Here the sound of trumpets is set ablaze, translated, of course, into bold and jagged octaves that hold on for dear life to the dominant. Then, rather unexpectedly, a *fortissimo* reentry of the Dies Irae, now transformed into a somewhat more hopeful though no less agonizing spread of diminished chords (2:29), is interrupted yet again by the trumpet calls before dissolving gently into an A-flat seventh chord (2:50). The texture then thins, giving leave once again to the Dies Irae to resume its original design, albeit in the darker alto voice (2:56). The ensuing moments are magical: still under the rhythmic spell of the Dies Irae, a vague and distant cloud of exotic harmonies—a bouquet, if you will, of a discreetly embedded, though enharmonically translated Neapolitan sixth chord (which is to say, a chord built upon the lowered second degree of the scale) and the subdominant (a product of the scale's fourth degree)—emerges wist-fully, as if waking from a dream (3:06).

As it attains self-awareness, an anxious variant of the Dies Irae in thirds and augmented fourths swells to *forte* in syncopes, only to die away yet again to *pianissimo* (3:19–3:35). Resigned, the ever-present Dies Irae holds court in the lower registers over a tenacious B-flat pedal, which tolls bell-like with the solemnity of a funeral cortege (3:35). In the midst of this final survey of the Dies Irae's now desolate and deflated world comes an anguished cry, a thickly accentuated *subito fortissimo* unable to sustain its last gasp (3:57). Its appointed time on earth van-quished forever, the Intermezzo bids adieu with the quiet and lonely ascent of an E-flat minor arpeggio.

Piano Concerto No. 2 in B-flat Major, Op. 83

2 Flutes, Piccolo, 2 Oboes, 2 Clarinets, 2 Bassoons, 4 Horns,
   2 Trumpets, Timpani, Violins 1 and 2, Violas, Cellos, Basses
Composed 1878–81; completed in Pressbaum, near Vienna
First performance a private concert with Hans von Bülow
   conducting the Meiningen Orchestra. Official debut of the
   concerto took place in Budapest on November 9, 1881, with
   the National Theater Orchestra conducted by Alexander Erkel
   and the composer as soloist
Dedicated to Eduard Marxsen

First movement: Allegro non troppo
Second movement: Allegro appassionato
Third movement: Andante
Fourth movement: Allegretto grazioso

Brahms wrote two piano concertos. As we have already noted, the first, in D minor, was the beneficiary of a number of ideas, born of his determination to compose a symphony, that were eventually cultivated and dispersed in this and other works. The D Minor Concerto evolved as a kind of symphony with piano, rather than as a vehicle for a virtuoso pianist to show off his prowess as he competes for dominance with the orchestra. Its first performance, on January 22, 1859, in Hanover with Brahms himself at the piano, was an unqualified success. But a few days later in Leipzig, all hell broke loose when an intolerant audience, unaccustomed to such bold, essentially abstract, and dissonant music, hissed and booed. As Brahms was still relatively unknown, the critics pulled no punches in trashing the work as "unorthodox, banal, and horrid."

Today, of course, we know better, and the D Minor Concerto has become a staple of the repertoire. It is also widely accepted and unanimously praised for the masterpiece it is. That said, I will move on to a more substantive look at this second piano concerto, composed some twenty-one years later when Brahms, by that time a celebrity, was fifty-five years old.

Brahms was on holiday in Italy when, in the spring of 1878, he intuited the first vague grains of this massive concerto. He set a few ideas to paper but declined to flesh them out, following his usual procedure of setting ideas aside until they were ripe enough to harvest. A few months later, he was back in Vienna, where he was entirely preoccupied with the composition of the D Major Violin Concerto.

In a fit of *Sehnsucht* (longing), Brahms returned to the gentle slopes and Italian sun, availing himself of the agreeable climate and full-bodied wines. But that trip, too, was cut short, and he was again compelled to return to Vienna. Evidently inspired by his Italian sojourn, Brahms reclaimed his old notebooks and set to work in earnest on his second piano concerto. Energized and inspired by his Italian experience, the concerto poured out of him like holy water, and of a piece. Even so, he continued to work on it for three years, never abandoning his own prime directive, that is, his preference for allowing his music to mature on its very own vine. Unlike the first piano concerto, this one met with a stellar reception.

It would not be overstatement to call this a mega-concerto. In some ways, it is not a concerto at all, in that it eschews, just as the first one did, empty virtuosic display in favor of more substantive musical values. It is unusual in that Brahms has penned four, rather than three, movements, interpolating a devilishly difficult scherzo between the massive first movement and the autumnal Andante. The piano and orchestra, while on more or less equal footing in this work, are not so much in competition with each other as they are engaged in a robust dialogue. Though this concerto, too, can rightly be viewed as a symphony with piano, it is distinguished from Brahms's first effort principally by the immeasurably deeper sophistication and maturity of the writing. By the time Brahms completed it in 1881, he already had a lifetime of experience behind him.

First movement: Allegro non troppo

The concerto opens simply and soulfully, a lone French horn giving distant voice to a broad, even earthy ascending melody in stepwise motion, capped off by a breathy triplet that segues over the bar and into a rising third. Only two bars elapse before the piano, making a fruitful and early entry, responds with a quiet B-flat major arpeggio that unfolds in an expanse of thirds, octaves, and chords before echoing the aforementioned triplet. A thin patch of woodwinds, dutifully harmonized, then takes over for a few bars before the piano again asserts itself in a majestic solo cadenza. Pianists have their work cut out for them here, as large, spacious leaps, cascading octaves, and emboldened left-hand arpeggios are configured in the service of an impassioned musical statement. Of particular importance here is a motivic cell that will be repeated or alluded to again and again throughout the movement; it comprises a short-to-long figure, configured as a sixteenth-note followed by an eighth-note, each lightly accented under staccato dots.

As this expansive cadenza comes to cadence on the dominant, the exposition proper begins. Here the full orchestra assumes the principal melody, now emboldened in a robust *forte*. The strings, in pursuit, assume an anxious new theme, set against a stream of triplets in the lower strings. The lowered third and fourth degrees of the scale provide local color and imbue its eighth-note pattern with a Gypsy flavor. Suddenly, a vigorously defined dotted-note motive—really a variant of the short-to-long figure made plain by the piano in the opening cadenza—marches in, carried by both winds and strings, with unabashed presumption, before a cascade of dovetailing sixteenths usher in a variant of the principal theme, now inverted in the winds against a chilly tremolo in the strings.

On the heels of two ominous trills in the strings in tandem with a broad salvo of half-notes in the winds, the piano resurfaces with thick chords and an alternating cascade of descending octaves. Oddly, these otherwise impressive events, which in the hands of a less inventive composer would merely become so much technical detritus, draw no particular attention to themselves, other than to the function they so amply fulfill: the prolongation of dominant tension en route to the tonic.

At last, the principal theme is given over wholly to the piano, which expands it into a rich procession of chords. Only a few measures later, the piano elaborates the triplet, enlarging it into strident octaves enhanced by a sweep of upward arpeggios, which, coincidentally, simultaneously behave like a complex appoggiatura. Another motivic fragment, which will take on special significance in the coda, rears its head in the violins. It is a simple figure made of only four notes: E-flat, F, D, and C, twice repeated. A vigorous dialogue between piano and tutti ensues, only to be interrupted by a ghostly, diminished chord, spread out and distended *pianissimo* over two bars in the piano. The flutes and oboes again invert a fragment of the principal theme, as the piano prepares transitional material in the form of an opulent two-against-three rhythm. The winds, not to be outdone, give voice to the movement's Gypsy-like second theme. The piano's response is playful, as it first assumes a two-bar stream of diminished chords. These debouche into a shimmering tributary of widely spaced arpeggios in contrary motion, vaporously accompanied by the strings and flutes. Yielding to an even wider expanse, the piano gently tosses quarter-note octaves at a leisurely pace across registers, and astride a pattern of slurred duplets, which conceal their real identity as triplets. Though only transitional, these motivic designs convey unusual spaciousness and grandeur and are further elaborated over the next six bars.

A shift of key from B-flat major to F minor makes room for additional elaboration of the thematic material. Here, the piano is entrusted with a magisterial chordal procession in triplets. Another dovetailing cascade of arpeggios moves boldly into an audacious dance, a pattern of sixteenth-notes, which march fearlessly forward in sixths and octaves. The nearly perfunctory string accompaniment merely purrs on, until it doubles up with the piano a few bars later. At this point the pianist's left hand engorges itself on an echo of the principal theme, now incarnated as a flurry of thickly accented chords modified above by a measured trill in double notes. The piano then intensifies the triplet figure, casting it in unbroken octaves against dissonant octave trills in the right hand. The piano rests its case on an F minor triad, at which point the full orchestra, horns and trumpets ablaze, assumes a variant of the principal theme, sending it into the minor and elaborating it with ominous regard.

The piano returns with the arpeggio salvo that ushered in the movement's beginning. At first this appears to be the start of the recapitulation, but it is in fact the onset of the development. Rivulets of arpeggios rise swiftly and consecutively against the pizzicato insinuations of the strings, which then lead into a variant of the short-to-long motive, now playfully set in motion by the piano in D major. A lyrical effusion of chords in dotted rhythms segues into a most unusual figure that, among pianists, has always been the butt of a joke, one hardly (or at least doubtfully) intended by Brahms. The figure in question is again configured as a dotted rhythm and bears a curious similarity to the "Battle Hymn of the Republic." As the key signature shifts back to two flats—a return to B-flat major—cascading broken octaves dissolve into a shimmering expanse of rapid arpeggios. These continue unabated in a plush *fortissimo,* then wind down to a whisper. The orchestral texture again thins to almost nothing, while the recapitulation is discreetly anticipated by a magical, tremolo-like figure that alights, in the piano's uppermost register, with the delicacy of a butterfly's wing.

After reintegrating the themes of the exposition, the coda simmers in a dark rumble of double trills in the piano's bass register. The pianist's left hand hangs on to the trills for some ten bars while the right hand gives itself over to a continuous, rising stream of broken octaves. Piano and orchestra then join forces with a renewed image of the principal theme, now strongly accented in *fortissimo.* The piano grabs the four-note transitional fragment of the exposition, hanging on to it for dear life in a rhapsodic embrace of enriched arpeggios. This, together with a variant of the exposition's Gypsy-inspired second subject, culminates in the awesome whoosh and blistering ascent of a rapid B-flat scale commencing from the dominant F. The strings, doubled by the bassoons, give voice for the last time to the movement's principal theme as the piano, flutes, and oboes envelop it in furious trills. Reinventing the opening arpeggiations, a torrent of alternating thirds swells up from the bass to the movement's victorious final chords.

Second movement: Allegro appassionato

Upon completing the B-flat Piano Concerto on July 7, 1881, Brahms wrote to his friend Elisabeth von Herzogenberg to report the good news. In a characteristic moment of self-deprecation, he advised her that he had composed "a tiny little piano concerto with a little wisp of a scherzo."

The insertion of this blustery scherzo into a concerto as massive as this one raised eyebrows in Brahms's day, including those of Liszt, who found the entire work "a little gray in tone." Liszt's peculiar assessment aside, it was the motivic material of this movement that Brahms once considered for inclusion in his violin concerto.

A forceful, even belligerent figure, given over to the piano, inaugurates this D minor Allegro appassionato. Its disarming simplicity is revealed in the form of four tremulous eighth-notes in pursuit of a D minor arpeggio. The entire figure takes only two bars to arrive on a tonic triad in second position, wherein its notes are arranged atop the third degree (F-natural) of the scale. With increased urgency, it gushes forth in a succession of mostly tonic and subdominant chords, two to a bar and configured as couplets. Each couplet is slurred judiciously in an effort to maximize rhythmic tension. The lower strings lend their support with a heavily accented stepwise figure as the horns blare out above. The mood is animated, combining uncompromising insistence with grim determination. A thick descent of chords in hemiola gives way to the first cadence on a secondary dominant chord, E major.

There, the strings proffer a second subject: a germinal, close-quartered motive that sighs quietly and orbits around two notes, E and F. In response, the piano assumes this motive and elaborates it with rhapsodic fervor, expanding it with chords and arpeggios for some thirteen measures before resuming, and then further elaborating, the principal theme. Here, the reiteration of this and the second subject branches out into an autonomous thematic fragment that rides uneasily astride a pulsation of displaced syncopes in the piano's alto and tenor voices.

The second, or B, section introduces itself with a reprise of the principal melody, now assigned to the winds, which surface in *pianissimo* and double thirds. Then the piano is distinguished by the dramatic appearance of the same motive, which here rises unimpeded from bass to treble with the inevitable air of victory foretold. The piano extends the motive, expanding it all the more in an ascent of alternating thirds and arpeggios. Soon enough, the piano and winds join forces, combining the duplet figuration of the principal melody, now assumed by the flutes, oboes, horns, and clarinets, with a patch of chromatically inflected octaves that likewise angle upward. With the reappearance of the second subject, the piano drops out altogether. But now the figure's tessitura is heightened by its inclusion in the flutes and the uppermost register of the first violins. The eighth-note motive then becomes an occasion for rhythmic tension, as it is doubled and thickened by the strings and winds en route to the bucolic trio.

The key now shifts to D major, and the tempo broadens into a more relaxed "largamente," which Brahms is careful to indicate. The horns contribute with a distinctive hunting call, a procession of thirds and sixths that move forward with optimism and assurance. Joined by the trumpets and winds, the horns bellow forth joyfully in *fortissimo* in a descending melodic fragment on the dominant.

The piano resurfaces with a diaphanous spray of octaves played *pianissimo* by both hands in unison. This unbroken octave string quickly morphs into smaller intervals of thirds, fifths, and sixths, before being interrupted by the winds. A passionate new theme emerges; it is a broad melody sung out by the piano over an expanse of arpeggios below. A transitional passage leads to a curious but effective refrain, wherein the piano mimics, with alternating octaves, thirds, and sixths, the horn's hunting call.

Finally, D minor is restored, and the principal thematic material of the A section is reestablished. Through hemiola, the imposition of accents on the weak beat of every bar, and phrase units of four eighths, the shimmering coda plays host to a hidden duple meter. This in turn engenders a tender contradiction to the overriding triple meter. The piano defines itself here in a perpetual, restless torrent of ascending eighth-notes, a variant of the movement's principal motive now configured in both hands as secondary dominant and diminished chords. These in turn, like kindling, set the coda ablaze and send it to its mercurial conclusion.

Third movement: Andante

Alongside the Violin Concerto's slow movement, this lyrical Andante stands as one of Brahms's most exquisite creations. Its embrace of the concerto's prevailing tonality, B-flat major, provides a welcome contrast to the stormy bluster of the previous movement.

A lone cello, impassioned and ardent, sings the now melancholy, now comforting principal theme that gives birth to this Andante. Set in 6/4 time, it is a melody whose contours held special significance for Brahms, who later recycled it in one of his most famous songs, "Immer leiser wird mein Schlummer" (My heart grows ever more peaceful). It extends over nine bars before the first violins, doubled by the bassoons and eager to command it, assume it. The cello is never far behind in this movement, where its presence informs affective nuance.

The piano's solemn, even magisterial entry, on a low B-flat, gives way to an introductory figure, a slowly ascending arpeggio that materializes as mysteriously as a full moon over an Alpine lake. A gossamer variant of the principal theme emerges almost imperceptibly out of it and, as it does, spins itself out in an unbroken stream of triplets in the treble register. These are set in subtle counterpoint against duplets, likewise configured in several voices, in the lower register.

Again, Brahms avails himself of wide registration to convey a sense of space and timelessness. This extraordinary melodic string, a nocturne of sorts, thickens into a vast polyphonic expanse of thirds and sixths before cadencing on an F major chord. Then, in a passage oddly reminiscent of the slow movement of Chopin's F Minor Piano Concerto, Brahms proffers a stentorian recitative of declamatory trills and arpeggios that then melts into a pulsating array of thick but deftly inflected, asynchronous chords played off the beat in the piano's treble and alto registers. The orchestral accompaniment is lean, offering the slimmest support in quiescent tremolos. The asynchronous chordal patterns, in tandem with the recitative figure, press on, amplifying the next fifteen bars.

The piano then reintroduces its introductory motive en route to an ethereal new figure in the remote key of F-sharp major; it is an enchanting Più adagio that again configures exceptionally wide, slow-moving intervals against a hush of pastel arpeggiations below. A solo clarinet, deftly supported by a slim gathering of strings, envelops the piano as it lends a certain otherworldliness to music that speaks so eloquently of regret.

The memory of his mother is said to have inspired the heartbreaking pathos that defines this music; indeed, Brahms alludes to another of his songs, "Todessehnen" (Longing for Death), a setting of a poem by Schenkendorf, and which he composed around the same time. ("Ach, wer nimmt von meiner Seele"—Who takes my soul?)

As the key shifts back to B-flat major, the piano moves forward with rare delicacy into a shimmering trill. The cello resumes its woeful melody and then enters into a tender dialogue with the piano. The latter conveys its consternation in an array of spacious triplets that move away and apart from each other in a lilting ebb and flow. The gentle affect of this contrary motion, though immeasurably poignant, expands further into a string of stepwise trills in the piano's upper register. Following their cadence onto a B-flat triad in the penultimate measure, this moving Andante draws to a close with an echo of the ascending arpeggio that gave birth to the opening measures of the concerto.

Fourth movement: Allegretto grazioso

The finale of the B-flat concerto is nothing if not insouciant, its ingratiating and cheerful melody imbued with just a touch of melancholy. Even so, it satisfies its concept as a rondo as it evokes the sweet strains of a Gypsy violin. This is a playful but consistent work that proceeds in four-bar phrase units. Indeed, its principal theme prospers by means of the lightly inflected iambic motive that informs it.

Brahms spins and varies the gracious dance that propels the music forward, though he is careful to keep the texture transparent and uncluttered. The orchestra's role is largely supportive, taking its cue, for the most part, from the thematic material first introduced by the piano. That in itself points to a certain role reversal, as the solo part of a concerto was traditionally subservient, at least where the assimilation of melody goes, to the orchestra's lead.

In any case, after the piano has had its say, the violins take over the principal melody for a while until the emergence of a new section. Though the key signature here shifts to one flat, thus suggesting F major, it begins, with characteristic ambiguity, in A minor. Here, an allusion to the second movement's principal subject is set forth by the woodwinds, which transform it into an exotic bit of zigeuner (Gypsy) matter, accompanied by the piano's somewhat strident triplet undulations. Following this, F major establishes itself, and the piano launches a quiet sighing motive, capped off by a round of triplets, six to a bar, in thirds and sixths.

On their heels is another derivative motivic fragment, likewise attributable to the second movement's principal subject. The mood lightens as the thematic material is transformed into a rush of ascending triplets configured in double thirds, and then a puckish spray of sixteenths in octave unisons. The home key of B-flat major is restored to prominence, but only briefly, en route to D major, where Brahms uses the piano to combine and intensify the principal themes in hemiola. Then, for a brief while, the piano vanishes and the winds and strings tumble one over the other in imitation. The piano resumes its duties soon enough, but with an air of consternation set forth in rapid arpeggios and the chromatic ascent in octaves of a variant of the principal theme. An evocative cadenza, meticulously written out in slurred sixths and thirds, suggests the lingering slides and glissandi of a violinist playing double-stops.

Returning to B-flat major yet again, Brahms revisits each of the thematic fragments in their various incarnations. A particularly treacherous, rapidly ascending scale in double thirds presents a special challenge for the pianist, who is obliged to play it affectively and in time. The brisk, joyful dialogue that ensues between the piano and the entire orchestra marshals its forces en route to the coda. An audacious chordal passage embodies within it a stomping Gypsy dance; some sixty years later, Dmitry Shostakovich would allude to this passage in his First Piano Concerto.

The tempo accelerates at the entry of the coda, which flies by in a devilish sprint of octaves that is perhaps more Italian than Hungarian; it is more on the order of a tarantella. The pace again accelerates as the texture thickens; the strings regurgitate the rhythmic design of the principal theme without duplicating the melody. The piano toys coyly with the orchestra, as if it were a naughty lover, and a dazzling parade of octaves and double notes dances over the entire range of the keyboard. As the piano celebrates itself in glittering arpeggios, this remarkable concerto comes to a festive end.

Violin Concerto in D Major, Op. 77

Solo Violin, 2 Flutes, 2 Oboes, 2 Clarinets, 2 Bassoons, 4 Horns, 2 Trumpets, Timpani, Violins 1 and 2, Violas, Cellos, Basses

Composed in 1877 in Portschach, Austria

Premiere at the Gewandhaus in Leipzig, January 1, 1877, with violinist Joseph Joachim, Brahms conducting

Dedicated to Joseph Joachim

First movement: Allegro non troppo
Second movement: Adagio
Third movement: Allegro giocoso, ma non troppo vivace—
  Poco più presto

Brahms is certainly not the first composer to have his work dubbed "unplayable" by a celebrated soloist of his own era. Indeed, much the same was said about Tchaikovsky's now famous B-flat Minor Concerto—even Anton Rubinstein, to whom it was dedicated, refused to play it.

Things were no different in the case of the Brahms D Major Violin Concerto. Hans von Bülow, the conductor, pianist, and Liszt protégé who often had kind and supportive words for Brahms, took aim at the composer on this occasion, claiming the work was not for the violin, but "against the violin." Elsewhere, two of the most celebrated violinists of the era, Henryk Wieniawski and Pablo de Sarasate, labeled it unworthy of attention, as it was—you guessed it—"unplayable." Sarasate, unconvinced of the work on musical grounds, complained that the oboe "played the only melody in the piece."

This august concerto, the only one Brahms wrote for the violin—and composed in the very same year that Tchaikovsky penned his own concerto in the genre—has long since become a staple of the mainstream repertoire. No violinists worth their salt can afford to ignore it, as that would say a great deal more about the violinists than it would about Brahms. Though it certainly is not the only virtuoso music Brahms ever composed for the violin—his chamber music and, of course, the three violin sonatas are hefty assignments in their own right, requiring a player of uncommon skill and interpretive insight—it is perhaps the most taxing and complex.

Performers capable of rising to the heights demanded by this concerto know well that their command of the instrument, if they are to do the work justice, must be comprehensive, at the very least. In spite of the key in which it is written, which allows a fiddler to exploit the sympathetic vibrations of the open strings on the instrument, its technical and interpretive challenges are abundant. Multiple double-stops (wherein the player must execute two or more notes on one or more strings simultaneously), lightning-swift but sometimes lighter-than-air arpeggiations and scale passages, a broad and frequently shifting range of dynamics, and complex rhythmic patterns all combine to make an effective and meaningful performance of this chestnut exceptionally difficult.

Brahms was fortunate to have Joseph Joachim, a loyal and devoted friend and colleague, as the work's chief protagonist. Joachim, who was two years older than Brahms, befriended the composer in 1853, at the time he was composing the F Minor Piano Sonata. Brahms thought nothing of asking Joachim for his advice and criticism, sending him only the solo part, perhaps in the hope that he'd simply imagine what the orchestral score was like.

Joachim was not only a highly regarded and internationally famous violinist, but a composer, as well, whose own violin concerto, the "Hungarian," was a model for Brahms, though perhaps not so much as Beethoven's far more famous concerto. Though no thematic relationship links the two concertos, Joachim's effort in the genre, which he based to a large extent on Beethoven's Third Piano Concerto, was a long and drawn-out affair, significant for its contribution to the literature and to violin technique, but also long-winded and not especially memorable. One can only imagine what Joachim, upon hearing his friend's work, must have intuited. Already well aware and firmly convinced of

Brahms's genius, he must have known, at least intuitively, that the D Major Concerto would long outlive his own. "It is a great, sincere joy for me that you are writing a violin concerto," he wrote Brahms upon receiving the score. "Some parts have quite an original violinistic flair."

If the understatement implicit in that remark rings like a matter of pride, Joachim's sincerity was never in doubt. Even so, while the "Hungarian" concerto is rarely performed now, the Brahms D Major is proffered, recorded, and broadcast every day the world over. Brahms originally composed four movements but jettisoned two, replacing them with the poignant adagio that we know today.

I would be remiss were I not to shine some light on Ginette Neveu, the great French violinist who is featured on the accompanying CD. Neveu, who died tragically in a plane crash in the Andes shortly after recording the Brahms concerto in 1949, was among a handful of performers whose mastery of this work rose to the sublime. She was a most uncommon musician, one whose intellectual probity and interpretive wisdom were matched by a free spirit and an open heart. Her sensibility, so perfectly suited to this music, is at times unnerving for the uncanny intuition she demonstrates at every moment, as if she was not a performer at all, nor even playing an instrument, but was simply a messenger for some higher power. Indeed, there is a disembodied quality about her playing. In this performance, Brahms's music seems to materialize on its own, and with exquisite finesse.

First movement: Allegro non troppo

It doesn't take Brahms long to establish the majority of his motivic ideas. Indeed, in this concerto the introduction, which gives sanctuary to most of them, is an extended affair, considerably longer than most other concertos in the genre. In contradiction to the Second Piano Concerto, which Brahms was also working on at the same time and which sends the pianist right into the fray at its beginning, here the soloist is compelled to wait.

That the bassoons, violas, and cellos are assigned the first salvo of this fiery Allegro non troppo, a work in sonata form but rhapsodic in

spirit, speaks volumes for the surprises to come. Indeed, these instruments, which are joined only a few bars later by two of the four horns,
sally forth in unison until the first half-cadence, where the remaining
horns and the basses enrich the theme in harmonization. The theme
itself is nothing more than an expansive, descending B minor arpeggio
followed immediately by an ascending D major arpeggio, each of which
are prolonged over two, then three bars, respectively. The mood is
quiet, even prescient. Only nine bars into the movement, the harmony
migrates briefly into the remote key of C major, giving weight to the
tenuous, chromatically inflected song of the oboes above, which now
introduces a new phase of the melody. Tensions mount without warning as the dynamic suddenly enlarges to *forte,* and any hint of C major
evaporates to give way to the dominant, A major. This transitional
passage, awash in hemiolas, sets the stage for the return of the opening
figure that now assumes an importance and energy that in its earlier
incarnation it declined. The entire orchestra, including the insistent
timpani, bellows forth here in harmony, though the strings have taken
charge of this already-familiar arpeggio motive.

But nearly as soon as it began, this now-invigorated motive gives
up its throne to make way for a new motivic fragment, which is on
closer inspection a variant of the oboe's phase of the opening theme,
now inverted. As the prevailing dynamic sinks to *pianississimo,* the
mood becomes mysterious. Then the flutes, followed by the violins,
articulate a serpentine figure in eighth-notes that extends, with each
appearance, over two bars. This motive, though only a fragment, gains
significance when it is later encountered, on more than one occasion,
by the soloist, who will recognize it as the elegant lead-in to a rapturous new melody.

But the introduction is not exactly out of new themes, either. Brahms
again values contrast, and here he offers an entirely new theme, a vigorous, harshly accented dotted motive assumed entirely by the strings. It
continues for only four bars, until the violins, already impatient with
it, launch into a furious drone of sixteenth-notes whose back-and-forth,
up-and-down motion mimics, in design more than in pitch material,
both phases of the principal melody of the opening. Here, Brahms
offers it more or less in diminution—that is, as an accelerated version

of its former self—as counterpoint to the woodwinds' tense harvest of ascending syncopes in quarter- and eighth-notes. The simultaneous emergence, too, of the timpani on a *pianissimo* trill just as the solo violin makes its entrance adds to the effect; the musical air is so tense by now you could cut it with a knife.

The entry of the violin solo is distinguished not so much by its breadth or its implicit virtuosity, nor even so much by its material, which is a variant of the principal theme. Rather, it is its overall character, which is further isolated by the near absence of orchestral accompaniment, that proves remarkable. The soloist is asked to play what essentially amounts to a cadenza, a virtuosic elaboration of a composition's motivic material normally reserved for the end of a concerto. From this perspective, the effect is not dissimilar to Beethoven's Piano Concerto No. 5 in E-flat Major (the "Emperor"), wherein the soloist appears in just that—a cadenza—at the very opening, and then again, after the orchestral introduction, materializes almost by stealth for several unaccompanied measures.

As the violin announces itself in huge leaps, double-stops, and migration across two octaves in a stream of continuous arpeggios, only the thinnest veneer of woodwinds and strings lurks in the background, creating more of a hazy sheen than a harmonized accompaniment. Even so, that sheen is deceptive; listen carefully and you will hear each instrumental section gently tossing the principal motive back and forth among themselves, as if making passive commentary on their efficacy. Elsewhere, the cellos alight on a single pitch, D, which they prolong as a pedal point for some twenty-one measures. The timpani, too, whispering in *pianissimo,* appropriate the same pitch for the first eighteen of those bars, intensifying it with a trill until settling on the dominant pitch, A, in the nineteenth bar. The soloist, who still has not been given so much as a moment's rest, rolls with the punches, drifting up and down from alto to the high soprano register in sixteenths and then triplets, for a brief spurt, before cadencing on a trill.

A fermata elongates a pause in the action here, but things quickly resume, "a tempo," as the soloist digs in with a flexible bow arm and even longer bowings to give voice to the principal theme, which is once again briefly restored to the lyrical line it once was. But even that doesn't last long; it is only a few measures before the solo violin again catches fire on a continuous slew of roulades, arpeggios, triplets, and trills. But the ethos of the solo part has moved from brilliant to impassioned, culminating in a brusque and immeasurably difficult passage in double-stops. Still timorous and sparsely represented, the various instrumental sections offer only the slimmest references to their foregoing motivic material as accompaniment to the rhapsodic and prolonged filigree of the solo violin.

The serpentine arpeggio that made its debut as a bridge passage in the introduction is now consumed by the soloist, who takes the lead with it en route to one of the most opulent and endearing melodies in all of Brahms's music. As if they cannot wait to get their hands on this lovely melody, whose raised fourth degree of the scale (G-sharp) lends it the quality of zigeuner (Gypsy) music, the first violins pounce upon it with an energy equal to that of the soloist. A particularly treacherous passage, at least for violinists, ensues. Wide leaps, displaced over the bar line in syncopation and offbeat accents, offer little time or relief to the soloist, who is then asked, by the merciless composer, to take up the bold dotted-note motive from the introduction, but now in double-stops.

In an odd twist, the solo part, not quite ready to abandon its responsibilities, and cognizant of its role within the ensemble, assumes the fluid array of rapid sixteenth-notes that the violins and violas carried in the exposition, just in advance of the soloist's entry. The mood becomes feverish; the soloist launches a tense ascent of octave double-stops, which transform themselves first into a brazen array of sequential triplets in descent, then into a torrential mini-cadenza, a blistering descending scale in pursuit of an equally bellicose arpeggio up to a high B-natural.

An ensuing cadence in A minor sets off the development, with a neurotic variant of the dotted motive passed between the winds and the strings against a pedal point on A-natural sustained by the cellos and basses. The violins and cellos revisit the exposition's opulent and still endearing secondary theme in advance of the soloist's reappearance with another variant, this time in sultry sixths and thirds, of the oboe's opening theme. The concerto's hue, darkened by this event, soon lightens under the marking "tranquillo." Here, the soloist proceeds with a graceful sequence of anapests—two sixteenths followed by an eighth—in a delicate dance with the now pared-down instrumentarium of strings (absent the basses) oboes, clarinets, and bassoons.

The tempo slackens a bit before the soloist takes on an ascending string of trilled triads, distended and arpeggiated. The strings and bassoons briefly assume the anapest motive, creating a quasi-fugato, only to be interrupted by the soloist, who again surveys a long sequence in ninths arranged in slurred duplets, wherein the stressed pitch of each couplet occurs on a weak beat. The effect is jarring, not only because of the Herculean technical command it demands of the violinist, but due, too, to the pungent dissonance these create. Just when you might have thought it would be impossible to turn up the musical heat, things intensify yet again when the soloist dons the dotted motive in octaves. A brilliant flash of arpeggios follows, leading to the recapitulation and the restoration of the tonic, D major.

Brahms reconsiders each of his motivic children in this fairly conventional recapitulation. Joachim wrote what remains the most famous cadenza for the concerto—Brahms declined to compose one at all—but that hardly precludes other worthy examples, less often performed, written by Ferruccio Busoni, Fritz Kreisler, Donald Francis Tovey (who boasted of his connection through Joachim to Brahms, whom he never met), George Enescu, Nathan Milstein, and others. More recently, the distinguished young violinist, Joshua Bell has invested in tradition and also penned a cadenza.

But the coda of this exceptionally rich first movement hardly bows out in a blaze of glory as much as it retroactively contemplates the concerto's own values. Indeed, as the cadenza dissolves back into the orchestral fabric, the soloist pays quiet tribute in a high register to the principal theme, now a shadow of its original incarnation. Another series of arpeggios, now shorn of their once glorious virtuoso bluster, passes by discreetly in a placid hush. Only the double-stops in thirds and fourths that bring the movement to a close presume something of the soloist's former triumphs, which have by now evolved into a distant memory.

Second movement: Adagio (CD Track 9)

In late nineteenth-century Vienna, the adagio had assumed a status
unknown a century earlier. No longer was there any hegemony of slow
movements, in which an andante was thought of in the same breath
as an adagio. Indeed, in the early, pre-Beethoven classical era, a slow
movement was a matter of preserving formal decorum as much as it
was an expression of pathos. But as time passed, it came to be viewed
as an emblem of spiritual potency and even religious contemplation.
No matter what elements they may have had in common, an adagio,
in the household of late romanticism, was no more an andante than a
greyhound is a saluki. Moreover, in Germany and Austria, the adagio
attained a peculiar cultural significance; its slow-moving grandeur was
perceived as an expression of the German *volk,* to wit, an expression of
the national soul. Adagios were no longer merely languid pleasantries
that took their appointed place in the middle of a composition, but an
occasion for both personal and collective reflection.

It was into this overall environment that Brahms gave birth to his
violin concerto and to this, one of his most intimate adagios. As Tolstoy
labored in distant Russia to put the finishing touches on the tragic story of
Anna Karenina, Brahms followed his own muse in pursuit of heartbreak.

Following a static two-bar introduction where the bassoons and
horns dwell on a tonic F major triad, a lonely oboe, delicately supported
by a light chorus of woodwinds, ushers in a simple but haunting melody,
a shepherd's song said to have been inspired by a Bohemian folk tune
(0:09). There is a subdued, if reticent, melancholy about it that sings
of sadness and regret. Assuming only the first few notes of the principal theme, the solo violin then emerges, some thirty bars later, only
to blossom with such humility and tenderness as to belie its material
existence (2:14). Indeed, as surveyed by the violin solo, the melody now
distinguishes itself as it attains autonomy. Rather than duplicate or even
vary the original, Brahms elaborates something new, positioning the
violin's yearning soliloquy in response to the pastel interjections and
occasional commentary of its instrumental brethren.

As the key shifts to A major, the tempo broadens, yielding to the
"poco a poco più largamente" that Brahms took pains to indicate. The

strings and woodwinds then proffer two bars of syncopated octaves and sixths before establishing a half-cadence on an F-sharp minor triad.

Here, the violin cries out in agony, its grief profound and its woes deeply engraved (4:02). Its wanderlust is that of a lost soul, its ethos that of devastating personal loss. The anguish is palpable, made all the more stark by its isolation from the ensemble, which offers little more than feeble, sporadic consolation. It can barely contain its suffering as it embroiders, with searing intensity, an expansive thematic diffusion over a two-octave range. Its desolation thus irradiated, it returns, some twenty-three bars later, to its native key and there yields to a single, ethereal moment. With its musical hands outstretched, the melody soars in *pianissimo* to a high D-natural, bereft, resigned, and abandoned to a fate of its own making (5:39). In the hands of Ginette Neveu, who makes of its fragrant nuance something exquisite, it becomes a timeless vision of the sublime.

Evolving from this celestial precipice is a ruminative emanation, a diaphanous descent of broken octaves that signals the onset of the recapitulation (5:51). These octaves form a dulcet, silky glow in the halo of the oboe's web, which again embraces the simple shepherd's theme. The coda plays host to the violin as it, too, adorns the theme, angling upward in heartbreak to a high C as if in search of solace it cannot find and as if, at that very moment, it had come to terms with the loss of the one being in this world it loved but who had become, in the space of a few moments, only a memory (6:46). Accepting its fate, its embers extinguished in sorrow, a delicate downward spiral of slurred couplets, in evocation of a sigh, codifies its fate (7:51). In the final measures it draws its last breath, making a symbolic ascent from the alto register to a high F, where all is peaceful, and where at long last it finds the resting place it so nobly sought.

Third movement: Allegro giocoso, ma non troppo vivace

In contrast to the previous movement, it is the soloist who launches this jocular finale, in 2/4 time against the slimmest accompaniment of strings. The principal theme, only eight bars long and played in vigorous double-stops, is a Hungarian dance of sorts that sports its audacity with uncompromising gusto. Here, Brahms may have been paying tribute to Eduard Reményi, the Hungarian violinist who was responsible for initially bringing the young Brahms to public attention. With the attitude of an errant Carmen, hands on her hips and roses in her teeth, this dance projects its devil-may-care attitude and asserts itself forcefully as leader of the musical pack. The full orchestra reasserts the theme before the solo violin again takes over, leading its charges with a battery of double notes that conform to Brahms's penchant for thirds and sixths. Like two old babushkas arguing at a Ukranian fish market, soloist and orchestra engage in a spirited dialogue, one interrupting the other as each vies for prominence. The soloist then grabs a string of widely spaced arpeggios by their collective throat, exhausting them en route to a sequential rush of ascending thirty-second-note scales. The tonality assumes an edgy patina, as the music has migrated, almost imperceptibly, from D major to E major.

Following a cadence on E, the violin sets the record straight and, as if to show everyone who's the boss, takes on a new motive, an ascending E major scale in octave double-stops, augmenting this with an impassioned response in dotted notes. Not to be outdone, the winds and strings, astride the nervous thrumming of the timpani in triplets, assume the energetic octave motive in an emboldened *fortissimo*. STOP! says the violin, reasserting its dominance with an identical repetition of the opening theme. An elegant parade of major arpeggios rises and falls, culminating in a new thematic fragment in G major and a new 3/4 meter, as well. This eight-note fragment forms a chain of falling thirds with a "tail," so to speak—four eighths followed by four sixteenths. Unable to make up its mind, it ambles back to 2/4 time, only to revert to triple meter again for another fifteen bars.

True to rondo form, every one of the movement's motivic identities then renews itself, though now in a spirit of cooperation with the soloist. The principal theme reappears, too, but this time given over wholly to the orchestra. Soon enough, the violin unveils an abbreviated polyphonic cadenza, ostensibly in 2/4 but really in a hidden, though unnotated triple meter wherein the weak beats gain an accent. An extended string of trills pulls the violin upward to D, before cutting loose once again in a continuous barrage of gruff double-stops and a bluster of arpeggios. After a prolonged cadence on the dominant, the violin, arpeggios ablaze, enters free fall into the coda. Here Brahms outlines a variant of the principal theme, making of it a rustic and wholly unabashed country dance in triplets (though here, too, the metrical organization is in six, save for the violin's imposition of sixteenth-notes). A patch of impertinent double notes in sixths, accompanied by descending chromatic scales played in unison by the winds, bring this remarkable concerto to its rugged, definitive close.

Piano Quintet in F Minor, Op. 34

Composed 1862–64

First movement: Allegro non troppo
Second movement: Andante, un poco adagio
Third movement: Scherzo; Allegro
Fourth movement: Finale; Poco sostenuto; Allegro non troppo

As we have seen, Brahms was often dissatisfied with his own music. What he did not burn, tear up, or throw into the river, he put away for future consideration or flat-out revision. The Piano Quintet in F Minor, which has long since become a staple of the chamber music repertoire, was likewise put out to pasture for a while, albeit in another incarnation.

Its compositional odyssey began in 1862, not as a string quartet with piano but as a string quintet. Brahms took to heart the friendly though informed criticism leveled against it by his two closest allies, Clara Schumann and Joseph Joachim; neither cared much for the way it was scored. Perhaps they saw in it some similarity to Schubert's great C Major Quintet and were concerned about how it might be received in comparison. In any case, Brahms recast it as a sonata for two pianos and performed it in Vienna in April 1864 with the celebrated pianist Carl Tausig. However, as thrilling as their performance surely was, it failed to make an impression, at least a positive one, on the public. Clara again expressed her doubts, saying she preferred the string quintet, and Joachim complained that it lacked charm.

Two years later, in 1864, at the suggestion of the conductor, Hermann Levi, Brahms reinvented it again, this time in the form most familiar to us today, a piano quintet. The two-piano version is still played on occasion, but rarely; among professional pianists it has proved perhaps more useful as a means of preparation for performance of the quintet, in that it allows a pianist to fathom and even absorb the full measure of the composition itself.

First movement: Allegro non troppo

For a first-time listener, the opening measures of the F Minor Piano Quintet might seem an enigma. That's because only three instruments, not five, play in unison. Absent from this initial presentation of the principal subject—which at the beginning of the piece serves as more of an introduction than the hardier embodiment it will shortly be accorded by the entire ensemble—are the second violin and viola. Even so, it is a memorable theme, a circular design of sorts that combines elements of the tonic and sixth degree of the F minor scale in a modestly distended arpeggio that cadences on the dominant C major chord. After a brief prolongation of the sonority under a fermata, the motive reestablishes itself in diminution, though now expanded by the piano, with just a touch of harmonization in every one of the strings, into a rapid stream of sixteenth-notes.

After another cadence on a dominant seventh chord (the addition now of a B-flat to the chord serves to enhance our expectation of what is to come) the ensemble embarks on a bolder, more confident presentation of the principal subject. The piano's role is largely supportive at this stage, complementing the texture as it does with fat chords arranged in broad, rather slow-moving arpeggios. The transitional material that follows is tempestuous as it appropriates the same motivic material in rapid imitation among the instruments and in accentuated off-beats.

A second theme appears, and, though its rhythmic and even intervallic design are nearly identical to the first subject, its character is very much its own. It is played by the first violin, while the other instruments, including the piano, provide a deftly contrapuntal accompaniment. It begins with a straightforward quarter-note followed by a dotted figure in eighths, before merging only one bar later into the identical motivic material of the first subject. A third subject is not far off. It follows a change of key signature from four flats to four sharps, a move that solicits, in this case, both E major and C-sharp minor. This subject, too, is a variant that combines elements of the first two themes. Jumpy, nervous, and uneasy, the strings carry it in contrary motion against the piano's unwavering bass triplets. But these outline a droning pedal point on C-sharp, as well as a rather mysterious eighth-note figure in octaves that rises timorously in the treble. The violas and cellos ornament things with their own variant of the melody, which has now been modified with an expressive triple on the second beat.

For the most part, the remainder of the exposition elaborates the principal subject, assigning the bulk of that work to the piano in the now-familiar flurry of consternated sixteenths. Meanwhile, the strings sing out in eighth-notes as they toss elements of the third subject among themselves. A whimsical sequence of syncopations enlivens the elegant, interrogative dialogue between the strings and piano that draws the exposition to a close.

The development, its air philosophical, is sustained by the violin and viola's meditation on the principal subject, accompanied by sustained dominant- and subdominant-quality chords in the piano. For now the overall atmosphere is at once quiet and contemplative. Here, the part writing becomes playful in a sequence of pristinely articulated iambic duplets, which swell from a distant piano to an imposing *forte*. Now the violin picks up the stream of triplets that the piano commanded in the exposition while the piano elaborates the dotted motive in syncopated thirds.

Eliminating the exposition's initial eighth-note presentation of the principal subject, the recapitulation jumps right into the excited run of sixteenths. The second subject rears its head again, but this time Brahms assigns it to the cello, which assumes its responsibility with a mournful wail. En route to the coda, the key shifts again, this time to F major. After the reiteration of the correspondent materials in the exposition, a hush envelops the onset of a reflective coda. The pianist has only one note, F, doubled as an octave and played in the bass for ten bars, while the violin and cello trace the principal subject in contrary motion astride the counterpoint and harmonization of the second violin and viola. The piano, having dropped out of the texture altogether for another ten bars, returns in an ominous ascent of triplets before resuming once again the now-familiar sixteenth-note incarnation of the principal subject. As if reassured, the full ensemble again reclaims the melody in eighths, asserting its primacy with heavy accents on the first and third beats of the concluding four bars. At the same time, the piano enriches it with a march of thick subdominant, dominant, and tonic chords, configured as slurred quarter-note duplets and likewise accented, but on the weak beats. The effect is jarring, but the movement nevertheless comes to a definitive close, and as it does, prolongs the tonic chord, with uncompromising vigor throughout the last two bars.

Second movement: Andante, un poco adagio

The essentially ternary form (ABA) that defines this movement depends for its life on the subtle embroidery of its motivic components. The piano introduces the principal theme, a placid and avuncular four-bar melody in A-flat major that proceeds in thirds. The strings, as well as the bass register of the piano, provide only a discreet accompaniment that essentially double the piano's bass line. It's evocative, certainly, of the figured-bass procedures of the baroque era, wherein an instrumentalist was expected to elaborate and build upon a simple ground bass or ostinato. But here the thoroughly modern Brahms leaves nothing up to the imagination of the pianist; every note is written out.

The ambience is calm, and a sense of ambrosial satisfaction prevails, as if to say that life is just fine the way it is. Even a charismatic new theme in sixths, again entrusted to the piano and carried forth in the tenor and bass registers, fails to either antagonize or challenge the abundant fulfillment expressed thus far.

The middle (or B) section migrates to E major and introduces a bucolic echo of the third thematic subject in triplets from the exposition of the first movement. Availing himself of his characteristic compositional vocabulary, Brahms positions the piano's response in duplets, thus setting up the ingratiating *Schwung* (swing) of a two-against-three rhythm, and he does so astride a dominant pedal point on B. As the piano moves into a passage of repeated octaves, lending the proceedings a sense of quiet determination, the strings usher in a shadowy variant of the eighth-note accompaniment it introduced at the beginning. The A section will return soon enough, but not before Brahms introduces a new motive—an octave leap, engaged by the cello and modified by a dotted rhythm. This motive is duplicated in contrary motion by the first violin and viola, as the piano accompanies them with a syncopated pulsation of secondary dominant chords, that is, a harmony that is the dominant of the dominant. (Keep in mind that the dominant proceeds from the fifth degree of the home, or tonic, key. Or to put it metaphorically, you might say that Mars is the secondary dominant to the Earth, though for a Martian, Mother Earth might have to assume that role.)

With the return of the A section, again cast in A-flat major, all the principal themes return, though here Brahms thickens the texture, entrusting the piano with fatter chords as he assigns the melody to the strings, as well. Enjoying their newfound solidarity with the piano's lovely theme, the strings press on in unison before going their separate ways in counterpoint in advance of the coda.

Indeed, the piano, not to be outdone, advances the cause of the leaping octave figure introduced at the end of the B section and, in so doing, echoes the concluding measures of the first movement. A persistent G-flat, the lowered seventh degree of the scale, colors the octave motive, now extended by the piano over nine bars. The movement's comforting second theme in sixths, as if in evocation of a fond memory, brings this Andante to its tender close.

Third movement: Scherzo; Allegro

Numbering among Brahms's more inventive creations, this playful Scherzo orbits around three motivic fragments. The first is rather vague, and not without reason. For one thing, the key signature of three flats, is that of both E-flat major and C minor. While the latter predominates in this movement, its role is attenuated by at the very get-go by the violin and viola, who introduce an anxious, ascending A-flat major arpeggio in a hemiola rhythm. Brahms organizes the first twelve bars of this scherzo in 6/8, rather than the customary 3/4. That, along with its coterie of iambic cells, lends it the air of a tarantella. But Brahms, who rejected musical Italianisms as unsuitable to his compositional vocabulary, declines to turn it quite into that. The pulsating pedal point assigned to the cello for the first twelve bars intensifies the texture, like a heartbeat stimulated in anticipation of its uncertain surroundings. What's more, the piano's entrance is delayed a full four bars, when it, too, assumes a chromatically inflected variant of the harmonic ambience.

As the time signature changes to 2/4, itself an affront to the traditional idea of a scherzo, a new motive surfaces in the violin and viola. It is a fearless, even militaristic dotted figure in repeated notes that rounds itself out with a tail whose contour, in both pitch and rhythmic organization, is a citation of the principal subject of the first movement. The meter returns to 6/8, and as it does, the third motivic fragment introduces itself. It bears the regal stamp of a march, its mood at once bold and optimistic. It is also yet another of Brahms's many allusions, which pepper his compositions, to the most famous motivic figure in symphonic literature, namely, the "fate" motive that opens Beethoven's Fifth.

Expanded sonorities and the reinstatement of 2/4 time propel all three themes into their uncertain future. The piano takes charge of the second theme en route to elaborating it, along with the strings, into a tense fugato, which culminates with the entire ensemble surveying the repeated-note motive with *fortissimo* intensity. On the heels of the return of the bold, marchlike third subject, the piano engages the strings with a belligerent hemiola that rises ominously in massive chords.

The optimistic trio in C major assimilates the Scherzo's third subject. The piano churns it out to the steady pedal-point punctuation offered by the cello. Though Brahms delays the entrance of the other three string instruments for seventeen bars, their participation is welcome for their enthusiastic duplication of the trio's now-familiar theme. Concluding its business, the trio segues into the A section, which is repeated verbatim, though a savvy ensemble will take pains to highlight different compositional relationships than it did on its first survey and disclose more of the riches this dashing Scherzo has to offer.

Fourth movement: Finale; Poco sostenuto; Allegro non troppo

Johannes Brahms was not one to forsake a good idea. Given its history, this quintet alone is proof enough of that. The octave leap that informed the Scherzo's trio sautés into a new body in this movement's expressive introduction. Each instrument, beginning with the cello, intones it *pianissimo* and with stark determination. Only thirteen lucky bars into the movement, the violin and cello emerge with an anguished and passionate cry, a broad theme that descends in quarters. The piano soon assumes the theme against the viola and cello, which in turn thicken the texture with double-stops.

On the heels of the introduction, the cello introduces a quiet and gracious new theme in stepwise motion that extends for eight bars. The cello is on its own for the first four measures, its folksy, dancing eighths and sixteenths at once suggestive and coy before the viola, wrapping up the theme in unison with a sprightly appoggiatura, joins in. The piano supports them both with a string of uninterrupted sixteenth-notes in the tenor register. However, what the piano offers is no mere accompaniment, but yet another example of a contrapuntal melody that implicitly embodies two voices. Its design is baroque, in that it takes on the patina of a fugue subject, without becoming one. Meanwhile, the piano's bass pokes and prods with single notes placed precariously on the weak beats. The time signature shifts, too, from a broad alla breve to 2/4 time. This shift signals a subtle metrical variant of the two beats per bar to which each time signature kowtows.

Things turn around when the piano, giving voice to the principal melody in thirds and then octaves, finds itself in league with the violin and viola, which have in turn usurped the sixteenth-note figure. The strings and piano, briefly migrating to F major, engage the principal theme as transitional material, only to jettison, moments later, any hint of the major in favor of a more bellicose variant of it in imitation.

Without warning, a new section, inaugurated with a stark, broadly distended G major arpeggio in the piano, rises to prominence. The tempo heightens. The violin, harmonized by its sister strings, sets forth a terse, rather anxious new theme in hemiola. Brahms sets this theme in contest with the piano, which makes every attempt to achieve prominence as it elaborates and varies the tune in an audacious array of rapid double notes, distinctly articulated in triplets. The strings then take a hint and try their own hand in this bold triplet variant, while the piano becomes ever more dominant, brusque, and even virtuosic. Not to be outdone, the piano demands its dominance with a slew of jagged, syncopated chords that, supported by a sequence of rising triplets below, descend with grim assurance.

A playful variant of the second half of the principal theme, punctuated by eighth-rests and in contrary motion, informs the ensuing section for some twenty-three bars. The principal theme surfaces in the identical incarnation that opened the Allegro non troppo, and with that, the parade of thematic fragments is revisited. In stark contrast to the syncopated chordal descent that also concluded the exposition, the piano emerges with a chorale-like progression. But it is not alone: an anxious iambic motive in rising thirds amplifies the reverent hush.

On its heels is a change of both key and tempo, to E major and "presto non troppo," and with this commences one of the more energetic codas in Brahms's compositional oeuvre. With its activity duly enlivened, the strings now assume a determined posture in a stream of eighth-notes configured in groups of five, which are separated periodically by eighth-rests. The piano retains its fondness for chordal progression until it, too, swept along by the strings, immerses itself in a continuous run of eighth-notes, all cast as spiraling scales and double thirds. With all the tension of a tightly wound spring, the entire ensemble presses forward. As the two violins echo the impassioned descending theme of the introduction, and the viola and cello thrash out their eighth-note pulsations, the piano heroically marches forward, imposing two granitic chords in every bar.

But even the piano cannot resist the swell of eighths, which the alternating strings churn out. Competing for attention, it appropriates the figure. The strings then turn to another, truncated variant of the expressive quarter-note gyration, which the violins voiced with such ardency in the introduction. The ensemble winds things down to a lean, quiet cadence, only to gear up again moments later for the final sprint to the end. Hemiola rules the day as dusk sets on this F minor quintet, which, now consumed within a robust and encompassing *forte,* concludes in triumph.

Ein Deutsches Requiem (A German Requiem), Op. 45

Soprano and Baritone Soloists, Mixed Chorus,
2 Flutes, Piccolo, 2 Oboes, 2 Clarinets, 2 Bassoons
and Contrabassoon, 4 Horns, 3 Trumpets,
3 Trombones, Tuba, Timpani, Harp, Organ,
Violins 1 and 2, Violas, Cellos, Basses

Composed between 1866 and 1868

First performance (of the first three movements) in Vienna, December 1, 1868,
at a private concert, Johannes Herbeck, conductor; official premiere, absent
the fifth movement, in Bremen Cathedral, April 12, 1868, Johannes Brahms,
conductor, Julius Stockhausen, baritone soloist; first performance of the
completed *Requiem* in seven movements on February 18, 1869, in Leipzig with
the Gewandhaus Orchestra and Chorus, Carl Reinecke, conductor, soloists
Emilie Bellingrath-Wagner and Franz Krükl with the Zurich Tonhalle Orchestra,
Friedrich Hegar, conductor

*First movement: "Selig sind, die da Leid tragen" (Blessed are they
that mourn)*
*Second movement: "Denn alles Fleisch es ist wie Gras" (For all
flesh is as grass)*
*Third movement: "Herr, lehre doch mich" (Lord, make me to know
mine end)*
*Fourth movement: "Wie lieblich sind deine Wohnungen" (How
lovely is thy dwelling place)*
*Fifth movement: "Ihr habt nun Traurigkeit" (And ye now therefore
have sorrow)*
*Sixth movement: "Denn wir haben hie keine bleibende Statt"
(For here we have no continuing city)*
Seventh movement: "Selig sind die Toten" (Blessed are the dead)

Had Brahms lived at another time or place, the words *Du fond de l'abîme* (Out of the depths) might have made their way onto the title page of his *German Requiem*. Indeed, some forty-five years later, a gifted and frail young French composer, Lili Boulanger, used that very phrase for a sublime cantata that exudes the spirit of Brahms from every one of its compositional pores. It was to be her final composition. Though *Du fond de l'abîme* went on to win the coveted Prix de Rome in composition shortly before her premature death at age twenty-four, it failed to capture the public imagination and has languished in obscurity ever since.

Nothing of the sort happened to Brahms, whose *German Requiem* likewise came out of the depths, all right—of his own soul. But to say that it is an intensely personal work is not merely a truism, but an understatement, given its rather convoluted history, a story that has certainly seen its share of interpreters and spin doctors.

Like so much of Brahms's music, the *Requiem* enjoyed a long gestation period, though nowhere near so long as that of the First Symphony. The origins of the *Requiem* reach back to his youth in the spring of 1854 in Leipzig, where he had been in residence with the Schumanns. In those days their young protégé was perhaps not as audacious as he was enthusiastic, to speak nothing of humbled in the presence of the two musicians who had become, in the space of a few months, his dearest friends and most forthright critics. In the Schumann household everything was music, and Brahms had at his disposal the three things a gifted young composer needed the most: time to work, distinguished and supportive mentors, and an inexhaustible array of musical resources.

His mind brimming over with an abundance of musical ideas, he set to work on a sonata for two pianos, a pragmatic effort given his proximity and friendship with Clara, who alongside Liszt was widely regarded as one of Europe's premier pianists. Though the sonata failed to satisfy his own rigorous standards, he nevertheless harvested it for motivic material that, as he correctly surmised, might prove useful for the future. A fledgling attempt to compose a symphony failed him, but no matter; something of the sonata would survive in the First Piano Concerto.

The sonata included a funeral march. But that, too, was jettisoned and its fate sealed when, in February 1865, he learned from his brother in Hamburg that his mother was gravely ill. En route there from Vienna, Brahms, devastated and inconsolable, could only hope he would have a chance to say good-bye. But fate cheated him of that opportunity, and his mother died, age seventy-six, before he arrived.

It was then that the various ideas he had been contemplating for his *German Requiem* began to coalesce. Investing with purpose the afore-mentioned funeral march, until then just so much piano music, the nascent *Requiem* began its long ascent to artistic immortality. It became the basis for the second movement of the *Requiem,* "Den alles Fleisch es ist wie Gras." In the months following his mother's death, Brahms was depressed but was also musically energized by her passing. Indeed, by his own admittance, it was the memory of his mother that fueled his determination to complete the *Requiem,* and he immersed himself in its composition in earnest in February 1866, taking it with him to Karlsruhe, where he remained until April of the same year.

What's more, some eleven years earlier, Schumann's attempted suicide likewise inspired Brahms to create a musical tribute. First envisioned as an indeterminate choral work, it eventually became the two-piano sonata, the very one that he later disassembled to become his First Piano Concerto, and also part of the *Requiem.* To make matters even more confusing, and doubtless because of the enormous popularity it eventually came to enjoy, Brahms arranged an alternate version of the *Requiem* for piano four hands. It was hardly a paraphrase, à la Liszt, but a literal transcription intended for private enjoyment or performance in the home. Now any provincial bourgeois could hear the *Requiem,* no matter if he was not sufficiently well-off to make a long and expensive journey to a major city to hear it in concert. All anyone needed was a piano, and some knowledge of how to play. Although Brahms was care-ful to include the vocal parts and the text, the arrangement is such that it hardly needs them. Indeed, he didn't drop a stitch, making certain that every note of the music was accounted for in the piano parts.

The performance pedigree of the *Requiem* in the first few years of its existence is nearly as dense as the number of women Brahms dated

and abandoned. The first performance took place in Vienna on the first
day of December 1867. The occasion was a private concert presented
by the Gesellschaft der Musikfreunde as a tribute to the memory of
Franz Schubert. Schubert, you see, never penned a requiem of his
own, and as fate always has the last laugh, it was left to a relatively
unknown musician to do the job. The conductor, Johannes Herbeck,
convinced Brahms to edit the work, leaving only the first three movements. As it was, Brahms had composed only six movements, adding
a seventh ("Ihr habt nun Traurigkeit"), for soprano and chorus, more
than a year later. Brahms was at first reluctant, as the venue was not
his first choice; in a perfect world he would have launched the premiere
in the overwhelmingly Protestant Bremen, rather than the stodgy and
largely Catholic Vienna. Besides, at that time he had not attained international celebrity but was only reasonably well established as the local
Kapellmeister of the Wiener Singverein.

Its reception in Vienna was mixed, though it inspired for a brief
time a spirited debate on its merits among academics and the public
alike. At its debut, an incompetent timpanist, unprepared and likely
befuddled by this unfamiliar composition, misread an important entry
in the third movement. He played so loudly that no one could hear the
orchestra or chorus. The Viennese audience, which to this day is as
musically sophisticated as it is a hard to please, would have none of it
and booed mercilessly.

It wasn't the first time Brahms had had such a reception. The public
hadn't thought much of his D Minor Piano Concerto, either, when he
played it in Leipzig some seven years earlier. But he was not deterred
and, taking to the podium himself as conductor, brought the still six-
movement *Requiem* to Bremen on Good Friday, April 1868. It was an
overwhelming success. The packed house of 2,500 included a good
number of Vienna's glittering luminaries, who are reported to have
wept. Clara Schumann, who was in the audience, had expressed her
love of the work some months earlier when Brahms entrusted her, as
he often did, with a copy of the score. "It is a truly tremendous piece
of art," she told him with her characteristic combination of admiration
and sincerity, "which moves the entire being in a way little else does."

The *German Requiem* made Brahms a star, establishing him firmly in the musical firmament of great composers. Thus it was a major turning point in his career. But he had one more major performance before he could claim his throne, on the home soil of Beethoven and Schubert, within the musical diaspora. In February 1869 in Leipzig, *Ein Deutsches Requiem,* as all Germany now knew it to be named, was performed in its full and final version, which included all seven movements. No fewer than twenty performances followed in Germany in that year alone.

But fame comes with a price. When Brahms, whose wit and sense of humor were nothing if not dry, reprimanded his friend critic Adolf Schubring for writing a perhaps overly simplistic analysis, his acidic remarks would not have amused anyone sixty years later. "Have you not yet discovered the political allusion in my Requiem?," he inquired, with a certain sardonic glee. "'Gott erhalte' was begun precisely in the year 1866!"

Well, "Gott erhalte unsern Kaiser" (God save our Kaiser) is a tune that made its debut nearly a century earlier in a Haydn string quartet. It was a catchy tune that came to be associated with German patriotism. While it bears a striking resemblance to the principal melody of the first movement of the *Requiem,* Brahms, who claimed it was merely coincidence, waxed touchy if anyone so much as brought up the subject. Even so, more than thirty years after his death, the Reichstag thugs of the Nazi era appropriated it (Haydn's tune) as a banner song at party rallies, where it held its own under the moniker "Deutschland, Deutschland über alles!" (Germany above all!). The Nazis, after all, were especially good at turning just about anything into a nightmare.

But in the late 1860s this melody resonated with uncomfortable religious and political innuendo, because in 1866 war broke out between Austria and Prussia. Prussia's objective to consolidate its population of Catholics and Protestants into a single state was shattered by a brief but ugly skirmish. King Wilhelm, under the guidance of Chancellor Bismarck, would later side with the Protestant Church to purge Catholicism, if not Catholics per se, from the land. In light of that development, the largely apolitical Brahms, who was pro-music but not anti-anything (save his disdain for mediocrity) became concerned that the "Deutsch" in the title of the *Requiem* could be construed as representative of his own political sympathies.

When asked about the title, Brahms expressed his willingness to rename it *A Human Requiem*. Certainly, though he came from a long line of Lutheran pastors on his mother's side, piety was never his strong suit. His *Requiem* was a humanitarian affair, one that proudly proclaimed that man was just as responsible as any God for making the world, and that of his fellow man, a better one. Brahms was in fact the first composer to pen a requiem that extolled such cosmopolitan issues as fraternity, eternal recurrence, reincarnation, and consolation. Unlike the Roman Catholic Mass for the Dead, with its reified body of traditions that demanded both the acknowledgement of Christ as a redeemer of lost souls, and the hellish price of failing to do so, Brahms's *Requiem* eschews such religious terrorism in favor of something more humane and unthreatening. Indeed, his concern is with compassion, and with comforting the living; he saw no point in punishing the dead, to speak nothing of their survivors, with ugly threats meant to instill in the faithful, as a measure of obtaining their obedience, irrational fear.

It is no accident that Brahms doesn't even mention Christ throughout the entire work. Whereas the Roman Catholic Mass demands the use of its prefabricated and pontifically approved text, Brahms fashioned his own from passages in the Bible. He had an encyclopedic knowledge of that ancient tome, and in selecting his own verses, upset more than one stalwart captain of the Christian status quo for asserting his independence. Whereas the Roman Catholic Mass proffers "Requiem aeternam dona eis domine" (Grant them eternal rest, O Lord), as its opening dictum, Brahms preferred the wisdom of Matthew 5: "Blessed are they that mourn, for they will be comforted," thus shifting the focus from death to life, from despair and fear to hope and spirit.

What distinguishes the literary content of Brahms's *Requiem* from all others is that the text, which he selected from Luther's translations of the Apocrypha and the Old and New Testaments, makes its own case. It is not a funeral rite or liturgy, nor even a mass per se, but an existential celebration of humanity. One can only imagine the reaction of the Vatican; it must have been something akin to attending a séance, where some pasty and bejeweled medium, eyes shut and hands aquiver, surprises her guests by demanding that everyone join hands in order to contact the *living*.

As for the title, *A German Requiem,* Brahms was adamant that "German" referred only to the language it was to be sung in. Of course, it also served to invest the piece with a certain autonomy, neither sacred or secular, and thus to distinguish it from the pretensions of the Catholic mass, as well as other musical works, such as Mozart's, in the same genre.

An amusing story: the Leipzig conductor Karl Reinthaler, who led the formal debut of the work at the Bremen Cathedral, feared a backlash from the legions of pious (to speak nothing of the Catholic Church). He asked Brahms if he would be willing to add a little something to it. What he wanted was a new text that both names and embraces, in a manner commensurate with the Catholic Mass, Christ the Redeemer. As the musical intendant of the Bremen Cathedral, the dour if not particularly imaginative Reinthaler had serious misgivings about performing this *Requiem* on Good Friday. Indeed, in a letter to Brahms, he expressed his concerns plainly:

> You come close to the perimeter not only of the religious, but even to the thoroughly Christian. Already the second movement touches the prophecy of the Second Coming of the Lord, and in the next to last the mystery of the resurrection of the dead. But from a Christian perspective it lacks the point around which everything rotates, namely the redeeming death of the Lord. You show yourself so knowledgeable about the Bible in the way you put the texts together, that you certainly will find the correct words should you find any other alteration advisable.

Undeterred by Reinthaler's not-too-subtle request that he rewrite the *Requiem,* Brahms's politely refused. And undeterred by his refusal, Reinthaler blithely threw in an aria, "I know that my redeemer liveth," from Handel's *Messiah,* all in an effort to please the theologically oriented powers-that-be. So much for the idea that cultural institutions were less susceptible back then to the extrinsic demands of pop culture.

First movement: "Selig sind, die da Leid tragen" (Blessed are they that mourn)

The *Requiem* opens solemnly enough, the chorus intoning its words of comfort, "Blessed are they that mourn, for they shall be comforted," fashioning from these an ambience so warm and sonorous that even the most casual listener would feel drawn into its maternal embrace. Distinguished by the absence of violins, the work paints its sentiment in the dark, autumnal hues of regret and sorrow that, at its darkest moment, discovers that hope is not lost.

Proceeding in expansive quarter-notes, the atmosphere is not gloomy, but empathetic, its burden only occasionally lightened by the strains of the flutes and a harp. The insertion of a destabilizing E-flat astride the tonic F in the second bar is in itself an act of prescience, or perhaps faith in what is to come; indeed, the anxiety is most palpable in the opening pages. At those moments when the chorus begins to sing, the orchestra, as if out of respect for what is being said, puts down its instruments and simply stops playing. This mélange of a cappella singing with orchestral interludes has the effect of setting each side—the choral and orchestral—within a frame.

The movement covets the simplicity and straightforwardness of a three-part form as it migrates from F major to D-flat major, a key that exerts an unusual effect on its listener's inherited expectations. As the lowered sixth degree of the scale, D-flat positions itself as a chromatic inflection that at once challenges our desire for the dominant, especially in the context of the chorus's overwhelmingly consonant harmonization. The interplay of these tonal centers in tandem complements the broad tempo and serves to slow time to a crawl, though not to a stop.

Soon enough, the chorus and orchestra meet on common ground in the work's middle section; as the chorus cites Psalm 26 and gives up its tears ("They that sow in tears shall reap in joy"), a harp quietly wells up below in triplets. With the return of the pedal point and the reprise of the principal themes comes a vision of recurrence and immortality. There is no Hell or brimstone here, but only quiet dignity, compassion, and the immeasurable faith of one whose love of humanity appears, in the space of this expansive heartbreak, even greater than humanity's love of itself.

Second movement: "Denn alles Fleisch, es ist wie Gras" (For all flesh is as grass)

Darkness prevails again as the orchestra sets the tone in B-flat minor. The work opens in a hush, the bassoons leaping quietly from F to B-flat, inaugurating a lengthy introduction. Sporting three beats per bar, the music at first emerges as a kind of funeral march. But that is deceptive. The wisdom of Peter 1:24, here intoned with heavy heart, consoles as it reminds, with unremitting fervor, that life is finite and death inevitable: "For all flesh is as grass, and the glory of man as the flower of grass. The grass withereth, and the flower thereof falleth away." Time is again suspended by means of the expansive tempo, as well as the imposition of accented upbeats, which swing under slurs and across the bar to unaccented downbeats. An almost imperceptible roll of distant timpani ushers in, at the crest of a crescendo and with inexorable intensity, the very same text, now sung out *fortissimo*. The motivic fragment astride which "Das Gras ist verdorret" (the grass withereth) is intoned is a thematic variant of the principal theme of the opening movement and thus retrospectively conveys the air of condolence and humility that Brahms, in music and word, invested so passionately in the first movement. Indeed, if this movement has any agenda at all, it is to convey, in both word and tone, the power of destiny.

The middle section migrates to G-flat major, removing us temporarily from earthly sorrows as the chorus pays homage to a higher power—for Brahms, a very abstract and personal one that needed no personification as it does in the Christian faith—which it cheerfully assures its flock is permanent, incorruptible, and loving. "Be patient, therefore, brethren, unto the coming of the Lord," they sing. The ambience is all hope; the words are set to a docile, thinly orchestrated *ländler*, a kind of symphonic lullaby that soothes and assures. No less confident is the chorus, now awash in the heavenly higher registers of its collective voice.

But once again, shadow supersedes light, and we are reminded, perhaps for the last time, that our destiny, already foretold, awaits fulfillment. Suddenly the skies clear, and they do so in the brighter key of B-flat major. Indeed, a renewed vision of faith in another kind of destiny now emerges in a blazing array of voices, trumpets, and horns. Here, faith bespeaks of its own "everlasting joy," assuring all who are willing to listen that sorrow and pain will vanish forever.

Third movement: "Herr, lehre doch mich" (Lord, make me to know mine end)

The return of the opening salvo darkens the musical skies once again, set against the distant murmur of the timpani. Reestablishing the tonic key, B-flat minor, a solo baritone sends forth the message of Psalm 39: "Lord, make me know mine end, and the measure of my days, what is; that I may know how frail I am." Set against a dominant pedal point, a shimmering patina of horns and strings imbues the baritone's inter-rogative with trepidation. At last, the chorus surfaces, echoing the same words. Soloist and chorus continue to alternate in a gentle dovetail of their respective parts. The baritone personifies transition—from earth to some other plane of existence—both musically and metaphorically. As the movement blossoms into major, he sings of the uselessness of vanity and ephemeral materiality, all the while navigating the musical waters en route to and way from the recurring, and ultimately stable, choruses.

A powerful swell of voices gives expression to collective optimism, voicing it in tribute to its God: "And now, Lord, what wait I for? My hope is in thee." As they do, the pedal point on D migrates to the lower, ever so sepulchral, regions of the organ, only to be surrounded, moments later, in the ambrosial sonorities of the basses, bassoons, and a tuba. The tonality has already shifted to the brighter key of D major; it has also given way to the establishment of a cantus, enlisted here at first by the strings, that becomes the subject of a robust and imposing fugue. "The souls of the righteous are in God's hands, and there no tor-ment shall touch them," proclaims the chorus as it takes up and displays its fugal banner. The restless continuity of the cantus, distributed with diatonic fervor among the voices and orchestra, might be construed as a musical metaphor, in that it provides sanctuary, not for dreamers or mourners, nor even the dead, but for those whom the dead leave behind. Indeed, in contradiction to a traditional Requiem Mass, which threatens damnation or demands blind obedience from the souls of the deceased, this work celebrates the faith and spirit of the living.

Fourth movement: "Wie lieblich sind deine Wohnungen" (How lovely is thy dwelling place) (CD Track 10)

Brahms casts this lyrical and exceptionally harmonious movement in E-flat major. It is a work that is as pristine as it is perfectly constructed, thus belying the complaints of his detractors that he was a musical reactionary unworthy of his exalted reputation.

The movement proceeds unhurried in 3/4 time, its lilting principal theme introduced by the flutes and strings. The chorus emerges quietly, intoning the text as the sopranos assume the principal theme in inversion (0:08). The mood is hopeful, as if satisfied with its unshakeable faith in the essential dictum of the *Requiem*: comfort (or "Trost," in German). As the chorus fades away temporarily, the orchestra emerges with an expressive thematic fragment, made all the more tender and endearing by the entry of the tenors, who likewise intone, in inversion, an expansive melody, inaugurated by an ascending major sixth (0:43).

Atop the quiescent strains of the clarinets and the staccato pulsations of the lower strings, the chorus, resuming its duties, assumes a nearly declamatory air as it gives expression, in dovetailing imitations, to its yearning text: "My soul longs, yea, even faints for the courts of the Lord: my heart and my flesh cries out for the living" (1:26). Those pulsations take on even greater urgency at "Mein Leib und Seele freuen sich in dem Lebendingen Gott" (My body and soul rejoice in the living God—2:00), before dissolving into the familiar thematic material of the work's opening (2:32).

Surprisingly, the movement doesn't simply fade away, immersed and satisfied by its own immanent gentility. On the contrary, Brahms propels things forward with a remarkably succinct and determined double fugue (3:40); the basses and tenor take the reins of the first subject as the sopranos and altos grab on to the other before reversing their roles some nine bars later.

A tumble of imitative voices comes to rest on a prolonged subdominant chord, accompanied by the strings in a hushed arpeggio (4:20). With this, the sopranos and tenors, followed by the altos and basses, enter with a compassionate, if broadened, restatement of the principal theme. The concluding six bars yield to the orchestral instrumentarium, led by the woodwinds, to carry the work to its ever-so-benevolent conclusion.

Fifth movement: "Ihr habt nun Traurigkeit" (And ye now therefore have sorrow)

Here the idea of comfort assumes a special, wholly personal meaning for Brahms, who, as we now know, lost his mother in 1865. This movement, as we have noted, was a late addition, and though its interpolation was inspired by formal and structural concerns, it was also, by Brahms's own admittance, a tribute to his mother.

The strings introduce the movement with a subtle thematic bouquet. Four bars later they engage the soprano, who is charged not only with inflecting the comforting words of the text, but also with embracing the listeners (or mourners) in the warm glow of her crystalline voice. The ethereal melody entrusted to her is at once timeless and curiously disembodied. Even in the shadowy umbrella of the accompanying oboe and flute, it is as if her voice doesn't intone the words as much as it floats them. "And ye now therefore have sorrow: but I will see you again" (John 16:22) assumes significance of a personal sort, too, for the aggrieved. It is, after all, to them this music is so eloquently devoted, as it so tenderly caresses them and pulls them to its bosom. The chorus, which materializes some nineteen bars into the work in a hush so solemn as to barely be heard, rekindles its faith with a single refrain that it repeats with each entrance: "I will comfort you as one whom a mother comforts."

Soon enough the chorus takes its leave, as the soprano, her voice spun like gossamer, introduces a new thematic expanse in counterpoint with the strings and clarinet in sixths. "Behold with your eyes, how that I have but little labour, and have gotten unto me much rest"

(Ecclesiasticus 51:27). But soprano and chorus resume their own labor lost, again alighting, with discreet confidence and thoughtful assurance, on the words of solemn comfort that endeared them to the faithful—certainly their listeners—from the very first notes.

Sixth movement: "Denn wir haben hie keine bleibende Statt" (For here we have no continuing city)

The apocalyptic tone of this movement, ostensibly cast in C minor, is fueled only in part by the text, which evokes the mysteries of death, and its promise of continued existence, albeit in a form unknown to us. Its uncertainty finds further support in the meandering harmonic mutations that destabilize it from the outset.

"For here we have no continuing city, but we seek one to come" (Hebrews 13:14) honors the transition between the world of the living and the realm of the dead that death itself represents. From this perspective, death is not to be feared, but to be understood. The restless migration from one sphere of existence to the next is codified in harmonies that themselves wander; the opening, which casts the meter in 4/4 time, eschews any relation to the tonic, instead positing G major in tandem with D minor, all the while prolonging suspense by delaying the arrival of the tonic key. Underneath all this, in the lower strings, is a no less restless, meandering progression in quarter-notes, which promenades in the halo of the subdued woodwinds. When C minor finally does arrive, some thirty-two bars later, it quickly changes its mind, moving contentedly toward the remote key of F-sharp minor.

Here, the baritone soloist offers, with stentorian authority, his prophecy: "I show you a mystery: we shall not all sleep, but we shall all be changed, in a moment, in the twinkling of an eye" (1 Corinthians 15:51–52, 54–55). At the "twinkling of an eye" (*Augenblick* in German), the baritone brings the music to an unexpected but pregnant pause. The chorus, its four parts tumbling one over the other as the tempo accelerates, then proclaims "for the trumpet shall sound, and the dead shall be raised incorruptible" as it shifts into 3/4 time. Informing this angular declamation, as you might have guessed, is a wave of robust sonorities given over wholly to the strings, brass, and timpani; indeed, the trumpet here is itself a symbolic emblem of resurrection.

As the music gains in intensity, the chorus challenges the very idea of death, undermining its power with the words "Death, where is thy sting? O grave, where is thy victory?" On the heels of a powerful cadence, the key migrates to C major and the time signature changes to "alla breve" as Brahms introduces a magisterial fugue. Its principal subject is introduced by the altos as they intone, with blistering intensity, "Herr, du bist würdig" (Lord, you are worthy—Revelation 4:11). This colossal fugue is virtually impenetrable as the chorus enlarges it to some 140 densely contrapuntal bars complemented by the orchestra's thickly layered and rhythmically propulsive sonorities.

Indeed, this fugue may be viewed as the apotheosis of the *German Requiem,* as a metaphor for the Word of God or, in more secular terms, for universal law. Resurrection is symbolically represented twice more underneath the chorus, as it were, as the lower strings, in tandem with the sepulchral tuba, move swiftly *du fond de l'abîme* (out of the depths) to airier heights above, some five octaves removed. The chorus invests the entirety of its vocal energy and spirit, inscribing itself with every fiber of its collective being in the words *Preis, Ehre, Kraft* (glory, honor, power). "Thou art worthy, O Lord, to receive glory and honor and power: for thou hast created all things, and for thy pleasure they are and were created." This is the moment of the apocalypse, the virtual denouement of the entire *German Requiem.* For Brahms the humanist, the "continuing city" of the Hebrews is hardly Heaven, a magical nowhere enshrouded in billowy clouds and angelic apparitions in creamy white togas, but the locus of human destiny and the essence of spirit.

Seventh movement: "Selig sind die Toten" (Blessed are the dead)

As it is in the beginning, so it is in the end. Whether that familiar saying is a biblical citation or not, I cannot say. But in the *German Requiem,* Brahms comes full circle. A sequence of rising duplets in the lower registers of the strings greets the sopranos, who, just as they did in the first movement of the *Requiem*, offer comfort to those in need of it, and even to those who would reject it.

Indeed, this ardent, ever-so-humanitarian finale is as much an actual transformation of the musical materials proffered in the first movement as it is an emblem of spiritual transformation. Drawing on elements of the first movement, Brahms brightens the musical ambience substantially through the addition of violins. Also, the swifter pace set forth by the ascending duplets, configured as eighth-notes, lend them a certain weightlessness as they drift skyward in opposition to the gravity of the opening "Selig sind" of the *Requiem*. Even so, this movement is essentially quiescent; it is only occasionally modified by brief dynamic swells, like the ebb and flow of tides.

Though Brahms indicates, at the top of the movement, "Feierlich" (festive, celebratory), the text may not, at first glance, appear to support such a tempo. "Blessed are the dead, which die in the Lord, from henceforth. Yea, says the Spirit, that they may rest from their labors; and their works do follow them" (Revelation 14:13). But *feierlich* has a broader etymological reach; it also means solemn, and an informed performance ought to be tempered by that meaning.

This otherworldly finale emanates, as it were, from the apocalyptic proceedings of the previous movement, as if to symbolize the dawn of a new consciousness, era, or spirit. The thematic, textual, and aesthetic parallels that link this finale to the first movement are not accidental, but a consequence of Brahms's convex imagination. Indeed, as much as future generations of composers in far-off lands might have tried to deny it, the influence of that single idea was enormous. In Russia, for example, where "mystical anarchism" was only beginning to take root when Brahms wrote the *German Requiem*, the idea of a new spiritual order, inspired and even engendered by music, was to become a defining factor in the aesthetic philosophy of so many of Russia's artists and intellectuals; they, too, absorbed and assimilated elements of Christianity into a fundamentally sectarian outlook.

Following an interlude in A major, the final movement of this, Brahms's only Requiem, slips back into its home key of F major. Its final moments, like those we all would hope we could afford to bring our loved ones, and likewise hope will be afforded us, bathe us one last time in its sea of consolation. Giving up its own ghost, the *Requiem* thins out in out in a celestial strain of woodwinds and chorus, embraced by a halo of harps, as it evaporates quietly into some mysterious, loving region unknown to death but anointed by life.

Appendix
Intonatsiia, or the Art of Listening

If there is one compelling issue that governs our relationship to music, it's the act of listening. Given the complexity and sophistication of most "classical music," passive listening is inadequate. To get the most out of the musical experience of listening, something more is needed.

In the Unlocking the Masters series, we provide ideas and even some concrete tips for music lovers to enhance their listening experience. This is why I'd like to introduce a singularly valuable concept cultivated and named by Russian musical culture. It's called *intonatsiia*.

Intonatsiia translates into English as "intonation," which in its more generic sense can mean whether or not an instrument is playing in tune. In Russia, *intonatsiia* refers not only to intonation of this type, but to musical expression. Therefore, I prefer to use the Russian word to help us think beyond intonation as we commonly know it. And for Russians, who learn the value of intonatsiia as children, it is so universally understood and accepted that no one even bothers to talk about it anymore. It's something one learns as easily as and with no less assurance than riding a bicycle. It's a skill that, once learned, is learned for life.

So just what is intonatsiia? Essentially, it is the codification of the musical tension that governs intervallic relations (distance between two pitches); it refers to dynamic tension, engendered by harmony and rhythm that occurs *between* the notes. This concept proposes an aesthetic connection between musical expression and speech. The aim of intonatsiia, as a tool of listening and performance, is to sculpt a musical gesture as it assimilates inflection. From this perspective, it is an interpretive device that allows a musician to illuminate the psychological dimensions of a composition and allows listeners to experience them.

The fundamental breeding ground of intonatsiia is the interval, that is, the distance between two pitches. Intonatsiia, then, refers to the attraction that one tone has for another. We call the nature or character of that attraction *affect*.

When two or more pitches are sequentially distributed, they form independent, identifiable rhythmic units, or motives. Motivic material articulates a work, informs its immanent character, and lends it consistency as it progresses. Motives are, in effect, the musical motors of a composition that drive it on. Angst, longing, tension, resolution of tension, anger, frustration, contentment, and so on somehow hemorrhage into music and find symbolic expression in compositional categories. In the rhythmic play of these tiny compositional motors lurks the source of all musical declamation: here music whispers, cajoles, rages, sighs, ponders, shouts, seduces.

This idea, which blossomed in the nineteenth century and came of age in the twentieth, has proved a rich subject for aesthetic contemplation. Take Mussorgsky, for example, a late nineteenth-century populist Russian composer; in an effort to articulate the concerns and psychology of everyday life, he saw an opportunity to create something more than glib program music. But a half-century earlier, Beethoven, whose works both developed and indicted compositional conventions and thus the status quo, likewise exploited the symbolic potential of music.

Of course, there is a great deal of room for interpretation in all this. What any individual musical work may "mean" is inherently ambiguous, and it is precisely that ambiguity that fascinated artists and philosophers alike at the dawn of the nineteenth century. The age of reason had given way to the age of fantasy. This development was in itself significant, because up until then, purely instrumental music was considered inferior to music with words, not the least of which was opera. At last musicians and the public began to see that maybe, just maybe, the violent sforzandos, dramatic pauses, and other dynamic devices introduced by Beethoven had something to say in their own right. What that was exactly remained to be seen, absent a lexicon or vocabulary that, like words, specifically defined what this or that musical gesture was supposed to indicate. This left the door wide open for musical symbolism, where suggestion and innuendo held court. The age of romanticism had arrived.

So what concerns intonatsiia, then, are not the notes themselves, but what occurs between them, and the degree of musical tension this "betweenness" signifies in their given context. Intonatsiia presides in the realm of intuition and bridges the gap between music and language, between artistic expression and social conventions. Intervallic space is rarely empty, but a kind of gravitational field where tones emerge, shift, migrate, collide, and resurface. Each pitch, from this perspective, becomes a point of condensation that absorbs rhythmic energy. Each note becomes "pregnant" with the one that follows. Working much like neurons in a brain, intonatsiia duplicates those sinuous structures; it is a synaptic process that telegraphs meaning across distance. Thus, once purged of words, which in speech and song play host to intonatsiia, instrumental music is free to give sanctuary to pure affect and inflection.

It should be noted that silence (rests) and distance, while properties of intonatsiia, are not identical to it. On the contrary, they are a measure of its inflective character and its affective potential. You might say that intonatsiia is to music what light and shadows are to painting: a means for determining perspective.

What occurs between notes, between phrases, and also between entire movements is dynamic, alive, and prescient. Musical space (by this I refer not only to rests or silence, but to the distention in time of a pitch or group of pitches as it expands outward, sometimes in stasis) is filled with expectation, pregnant with what is to come and redolent of what has just occurred. The compelling inevitability we experience when a simple seventh chord resolves onto the tonic, for example, or when a tritone (an interval consisting of three consecutive whole tones; F-natural to B-natural, for example) moves outward to a minor sixth (or inward to major third) is something we experience viscerally, even physically, in the gut, as it were.

The concept of intonatsiia requires the listener to develop the ability to imagine and to feel the progressive dynamics of a musical work with visceral intensity. In other words, we strive to relate to the life between the notes, and not merely to their vibratory properties the moment they are produced. "We create the necessary continuity that does not actually take place," opines Charles Rosen, who likewise credits the listener's imagination as responsible for filling in the gaps. In his view, "the expressive force of the music causes us to imagine as actually existing what is only implied."

In America, the art of intonatsiia has largely been unexplored by the listening public, who would most definitely benefit from familiarity with its principles. From childhood we are not so much taught to listen as trained to hear. There's a big difference, as the former concerns engaged understanding, while the latter assumes a posture of passive indifference. A large sector of the music-loving public is simply untrained in the context of listening. The good news is that it is not at all difficult to become an engaged listener; like any other skill, listening can be learned and cultivated. You might think of listening as a kind of muscle; with regular exercise it will become very resilient indeed. A specific means of expression—that is, a way of turning a phrase into something vibrant, plastic, and flexible, or a motive into something shapely, rhythmically articulate, and easily identifiable—can certainly be conveyed and taught with precision to any burgeoning musician. But average listeners, too, no matter their musical background, can likewise learn not only to recognize these events, but to distinguish their efficacy in any given performance.

Doubtless, some of you are familiar with the frustration of hearing students as well as professional performers who play flatly, without expression, as if the musical terrain were the cornfields of Iowa or the Dutch lowlands; there are no hills and valleys, no recesses and shadows, no mountains and vistas. Such performances fail to move us, because they are like one big canvas where every note and every phrase is played with equal importance. They demonstrate little if any feel for harmonic orientation, nor for the immanent tension and internecine dramas that fuel the work at hand. Absent, too, is any sense of movement toward concrete compositional goals, as if musical space were devoid of compositional events.

Intonatsiia cultivates an awareness of such events. From this perspective, each interval assumes its own character; as a general rule (but one that is hardly written in stone), the larger the interval, the longer the time should be taken to move across it. More often than not, that extra time can be measured in milliseconds—by no means does this suggest that note values should be radically altered or distorted. We are talking, after all, about nuance. Nikolaus Harnoncourt refers to these affective fluctuations as *microdynamics,* which in turn rely on musicians' ability to deftly characterize and shape even the smallest motivic units. And as they do so, we as listeners invest our own imaginative powers in the contours of the motives and phrase, following their trajectory as we perceive the manner in which they are organized and articulated.

Let's look, for example, at crescendos and decrescendos, those places in a musical composition where things become gradually louder or softer. What defines a crescendo or its opposite is not merely an increase or decrease in volume. On the contrary, what informs these particular compositional elements is a certain resistance to the occurrence of getting louder or softer; we discern their effect, as it were, by putting up resistance to the accumulation or decrease of volume en route to a climax. An effective crescendo or decrescendo relies for its power on the gradual distension and adjudication of its volume. Thus it is not simply a question of getting louder or softer, but of cultivating a feeling for those opposing dynamic forces that would stand in the way of reaching the high point of any phrase, that is, its goal.

This, by the way, is how a fine actor conveys heartbreak with persuasive poignancy: not by bawling uncontrollably onstage, but by making every effort not to, by attempting to stay in control and maintain dignity in the face of impossible emotional odds. In music, the same approach creates intonational and thus psychological tension, for in this context we experience the crescendo/decrescendo as a kind of overcoming that at once celebrates the gradual accumulation and ultimate release of that tension.

In the early nineteenth century, the notion of overcoming adversity and victory in the face of struggle emerged as a central tenet of musical aesthetics. Music, to a large extent, had become politicized, not only as a vehicle that was open to subjective reaction, and thus to any number of possible, if exogenous, interpretations, but also through subtle changes in the compositional process itself. Left to their own devices, rhythm, harmony, and form, while still abstractions, become ripe with meaning. Are the first, closely aligned four notes of Beethoven's Fifth Symphony, for example, really a symbol of "fate knocking at the door," as popular myth would have us believe? Perhaps. But in the larger context of the entire symphony, which recycles this motive ad infinitum, it may be that the four notes speak with succinct expression to the notion of determination and overcoming. While these are matters perhaps best left to musical semiologists, they are nevertheless worthy of contemplation, as they have significant bearing on the way in which we experience and relate to music.

The Grammar of Engaged Listening

It would be an oversimplification to say that *intonatsiia* refers simply to the differences between large and small intervals. Rather, it concerns the manner in which they, or any motivic configuration, are inflected and characterized. For example, *intonatsiia* can also refer to other modes of articulation, such as the way a musician enhances the opening pitch at the beginning of a phrase, perhaps by slightly lengthening it, like a skater pushing off onto the ice or a dancer inaugurating a jeté. This becomes, for our now shrewdly engaged ears, an impulse. It refers, too, to elements of surprise, suspense, and even violence (unexpected dissonances or syncopations, such as those that so frequently invigorate Beethoven or Shostakovich, for example); to the function of pedal points (the reiteration of a single note) to illustrate either stability or uncertainty; and not least, to the manner in which we perceive symbolic meaning. In short, intonatsiia embraces an array of expressive meanings that inform a work.

Intonatsiia encourages musicians to explore and exploit the expressive potential of every intervallic movement, to elaborate a musical grammar within the trajectory of a phrase, and to delineate and inflect carefully the character and shape of a motive. As listeners, we are equally capable of identifying and imaginatively engaging a work's many complexes of articulation as the music unfolds in time. It is the kind of listening that ought be cultivated with the greatest care, patience, and, I dare say, enchantment.

What intonatsiia produces is a mode of listening that migrates into every aspect of our listening habits and into a musician's playing. Here, expressive intent rules. Absolutely nothing, not even a scale, ought ever be taken for granted or dispatched mechanically, but should instead project a melodic attitude.

So far we've established that in its most fundamental sense, intonatsiia is all about what goes on in between the notes. It's something akin, you might say, to "reading between the lines" of a poem or a novel. It's the realm of affective inflection that conveys tension, longing, direction, and, on a subtler plane, the tendency of one pitch to gravitate toward another. On a larger scale, too, we've discerned that these same attributes likewise govern, though do not define in any specific material (that is, harmonic or rhythmic) category, the relationship between phrases, or even whole movements.

But is intonatsiia, when employed as a way of listening to music, in any way influenced by the instrument or the musical genre? Does it matter if a prelude of Bach is played on the harpsichord or on piano, or if Beethoven's Ninth Symphony is performed by a hundred players or by a far smaller ensemble?

Well, the simple answer is not so simple: yes and no. Thanks to the ability of every instrument *except* the piano, harpsichord, and percussion to sustain and intensify a single pitch en route to its neighbor, the average listener will at first find it easier to experience intonatsiia in orchestral and vocal music. After all, instrumental musicians provide much of the "synaptic" work already, filling in the gaps between the notes with discernible sound and volume. Whereas a pianist must convey pitch prolongation and intensification by imaginative means—since the moment any note is played on the piano, the sound diminishes rapidly—a violinist, an oboist, or a singer takes command of the material elements of legato, that is, the physical presence of sound in continuity; pitches hemorrhage one into the other.

Performers do more than recite or parrot a text. They engage it as they live in the moment; once onstage, they abandon nothing of their curiosity or wonder. And as they are doing so, the informed listener is likewise engaged. Both performer and listener are constantly looking for something new in a journey of discovery that refuses to reify music, that is, to turn it into something frozen and inflexible. Those performers and listeners who refuse to be intimidated by musical experience are also those willing to embrace their vulnerability to its charms and to admit that there is always something new to discover. Music, thus allowed to present its own case, is now immune from the kind of routine, passive, and thoroughly disengaged listening that would disallow it to move into our psyches and the fiber of our being.

Of course, as a matter of preparation, performers lay out a musical work in detail, identifying its structural elements in an effort to strategize the interpretation. They become cognizant of its harmonic goals, rhythmic trajectory, and the like. But by the time they go on stage, they must be free not to anticipate what's about to happen next. This is the responsibility of performers toward themselves as well as their listeners: to clarify the compositional prosody and captivate everyone's ears in the interest of fulfilling musical experience. Just as actors must "find" the words of the script as if they'd never read or heard them before, so must musicians find the notes anew as they looks behind, between, and beyond them for meaning.

The French philosopher Roland Barthes described this process as "inscribing" oneself in the text, wherein reading is no less an active engagement than writing. Ideally, we should "write" what we read, reinventing the text as we "inscribe" ourselves dialectically within it. In so doing, we dissolve barriers that would otherwise separate the one activity from the other. And thus as listeners, too, we strive to participate in music in ways that are just as significant and intense as performers' engagement with the work.

To hear music is not enough; in order to gain the most from the experience, to satisfy our curiosity and whet our sensual appetites, we should heed Theodor W. Adorno's advice and listen along with the music. While there is no compelling need for listeners to identify any particular compositional event by its technical name (which would assume a level of training that most listeners do not have), we can, however, cultivate sensitivity to musical "events," that is, to those things in the musical text that jar, move, or strike us as strange. To paraphrase Barthes, we inscribe ourselves individually in the music.

Intonatsiia, then, may provide a key to understanding, listening, and performing music in the context of the conventions of the composer's era, and in accordance with his aesthetic philosophy as well as our own.

Glossary

accelerando   A gradual heightening or cumulative quickening of tempo.

adagio   A slow tempo, but neither turgid nor comatose. An adagio must move, broadly.

affect   Comes from the *Affektenlehre*, or "Doctrine of Affects," a seventeenth-century aesthetic ideology holding that the emotions could be codified in sound and that a rhetorical grammar of such affections could be made part of compositional procedure. Though not exactly interchangeable in our use of the terms, it is a species of *inflection* and is best described as referring to the degree of emphasis, dynamic weight, or perspective performers invest in any given motivic figuration.

allegretto   A lively, quick, and above all playful tempo, but not quite so fast as allegro.

allegro   Generally understood to be a fast or moderately fast tempo, but in music of the baroque and classical eras, especially, it refers to character and disposition; it can be construed to mean "cheerful" or "happy."

andante   A gracious, walking tempo, not too slow nor too quick. Subject to any number of gradations.

articulation   The manner in which a performer distinguishes (by means of attack, prolongation, and release) certain tones, motives, phrases, and groups of pitches individually and in relation to each other. Composers either spell out or provide symbols to indicate types of articulation, such as staccato, legato, wedges, tenuto, and other accent marks.

baroque music   Music composed roughly between 1590 and 1750 and that embraces certain styles and techniques attributable to the aesthetic ideas, formulations, and philosophy of the era. Because of its long run, it is usually divided into three distinct subperiods, each governed by specific innovations. Opera, the fugue, and the harmonization of a ground bass were products of baroque invention.

cadence   A harmonic progression that demarcates the end of a phrase or larger section of a work and provides a sense of resolution, with varying degrees of finality. In its harmonic tendency to move back toward the key of the work, cadence is also an expression of a composition's tonality.

cadenza   An extended solo passage usually, but not only, found in a concerto. It typically comes toward the end of a concerto or sonata form movement, before the coda, and it elaborates and ornaments the principal themes of the work with a view toward showing off the skill of its composer or soloist, or both. Though composers sometimes write out the cadenza, performers, too, occasionally write their own.

canon   A musical pattern defined by a thematic subject that is presented, then successively imitated by one or more voices commencing on different pitches. There are different kinds of canon: fixed, which is imitation by rote; and free, which introduces modifications of pitch material and rhythm.

capriccio   The character actor of musical composition, usually a piece that is defined by its bizarre, agitated, and humorous qualities and that favors abrupt and often radical contrasts, both rhythmic and harmonic.

classical era   The period of musical composition that extended from the early eighteenth through the early nineteenth centuries. Its exact division into years is difficult to measure, as classicism evolved slowly and its attendant techniques and aesthetics eventually bled into romanticism. Characteristics of music of the classical era include periodic phrasing; longer harmonic rhythms; a prevalence of simpler, more natural melodic designs; homophonic textures; and greater use of specifically marked dynamic contrasts.

coda   The concluding section of a movement or single composition that usually encapsulates the work's principal themes. A coda may be as brief as a few measures, or elaborate and extensive.

counterpoint   The simultaneous unfolding of two or more melodies, and the various compositional principles that govern their existence and formulation—that is, their movement apart or away from each other, their rhythmic differences, and the resultant harmonies they create in relation to each other.

crescendo,   A gradual, cumulative increase or decrease in
decrescendo   volume indicated by hairpin signs or written out as a word by the composer. This intensification of sound in either direction informs the affective character of the passage it modifies.

development   The middle section of a movement in sonata form wherein the principal themes and motivic ideas are varied, elaborated, intensified, ornamented, en route to the recapitulation.

Dies Irae   Latin for "Day of Wrath", the Dies Irae is a rhymed sequence whose origins go back to the fourteenth century. Formally designated by the Catholic

Church as part of the Requiem Mass in the six-teenth century, the stark and ominous series of seven notes that identify it have endeared it to generations of composers who have favored it as a cantus firmus, a thematic subject for variation treat-ment, or a symbolic interjection to signify death.

diminution   The presentation of a melody in note values shorter than those in which it was originally cast.

dominant   Every major and minor scale consists of seven pitches; the fifth scale degree is called the *dominant*. A chord constructed around this pitch includes the seventh degree of the scale. The tendency of the seventh degree to move toward its neighboring tonic pitch is strong and creates in listeners a feeling of strong expectation and desire for resolution.

dotted notes   A dot placed just alongside a pitch increases the tem-poral value of that note by one half of its original value. Two dots set in this way increase the value by yet another quarter of that value.

exposition   The first section of a sonata, in which the princi-pal themes of the compositions are presented in juxtaposition one to the other, and which includes at least one major modulation to a secondary key, most often, but not necessarily, the dominant.

forte; fortissimo   Loud; very loud (though best interpreted as "strong; very strong").

fugue   A composition in which a theme (also known as a *sub-ject*) is stated and then repeated consecutively in two or more voices in imitative counterpoint. This con-fluence of voices is then elaborated, extended, varied, modulated, or developed in any number of ways.

fugato	A usually brief contrapuntal section that occurs within a sonata movement or other form and that does not develop into a full-blown fugue, although it is at once contrapuntal and imitative (the essential characteristics of a fugue).
hemiola	A kind of rhythmic substitute, wherein two measures in triple meter are both notated and played as if they were three bars in duple meter.
intonatsiia	A Russian concept that defines intervallic relationships, referring to and codifying the implicit musical tension, both rhythmic and dynamic, that we experience *between* any two pitches in a motive or melody. On a larger scale, it also governs transitions that link larger phrase units. Intonatsiia is the musical equivalent of a neuron, functioning as a conduit that carries musically relevant information such as rhythm, nuance, and dynamic tendencies from one pitch to another.
intermezzo	Originally a brief comic interlude set between acts of an opera, in the nineteenth century it became a short and lyrical character piece that stood on its own in instrumental music.
larghetto	Not quite so slow as largo.
lento	Slow.
menuetto (*minuet*)	An elegant dance in 3/4 time that had its origins in seventeenth-century France. It is usually in two-part (binary) form, and its second beats are often accented. When danced, the minuet was a little slower than when performed strictly as instrumental music.
motive, motif	A brief rhythmic unit of a specific duration and design that acquires its own identity and becomes

the basis of more elaborate structures, movements, and whole works.

Neapolitan sixth   A chromatically inflected inverted triad (that is, one with the third at the bottom rather than in the middle) that is based on the lowered second degree of the scale; it can be major or minor. In C major, the Neapolitan sixth is based on D-flat, with F-natural as the lowest pitch.

ostinato   A repetitive rhythmic and melodic pattern reiterated over the course of a composition, usually carried in the bass.

passacaglia   A form, originating in the baroque era, consisting of a string of uninterrupted variations over a recurring bass line.

pedal point   A single tone, reiterated and sustained under changing harmonic patterns and over an extended period. While pedal points frequently occur in the bass, they can also be dispatched in any voice to enhance harmonic and rhythmic tension.

piano; pianissimo   Soft; very soft.

più animato   More animated, livelier.

pizzicato   For stringed instruments, an articulation wherein the string is plucked with the fingers rather than bowed.

polyphony   Wherein several musical voices, or lines, are heard in combination, and where each line has an independent character.

presto; prestissimo   Very fast; faster still than presto.

recapitulation   In sonata form, the concluding section of a movement, wherein all the principal themes of the work are restated, usually in the tonic key.

rallentando   Increasingly slower.

ritardando	Slowing down.
rondo	A form in several sections, wherein the principal section (A) alternates with subsequent sections (B, C, D, etc.). Whenever the principal (A) section is restated, it is usually in the tonic key.
scherzo	A light, playful, even mischievous dance form that in the late eighteenth and nineteenth centuries often replaced the minuet as a movement in symphonies and in instrumental music. It is played swiftly in 3/4 time and includes a contrasting trio section.
sforzando	A sudden, interruptive accentuation.
sonata form	The traditional form used most often in the first movements of instrumental music from the classical period and beyond. Though it can be identified by a few standard organizational procedures—exposition, development, and recapitulation, as well as key relationships that juxtapose tonic and dominant in the first section, and so on—it is best viewed as a dynamic process.
staccato	The distinct separation of a pitch from its neighboring notes. From the baroque era onward, staccato was an articulation marking, indicated by a dot above the note that instructed the player to cancel the prevailing legato.
stringendo	A tempo instruction indicating that a passage should become progressively faster.
subdominant	Refers to a pitch, chord, or tonality based on the fourth degree of a major or minor scale.
syncope (short for *syncopation*)	A temporary shift of accent that contradicts the metrical organization within a bar line or phrase, though the metrical identity of he passage stays intact. For example, an accent on a weak beat of a bar on the heels of unaccented strong beat will

modify the function of those beats, turning a weak beat into a strong beat, and can thus affect harmonic orientation, articulation, and rhythmic trajectory.

tempo   The rate of speed at which a piece of music is played; a specific tempo is indicated by the composer, who relies on a performer to respect his instructions according to the universally understood precepts, and in accordance with contemporary performance practice.

tonality   The organization of tones around a single central pitch, or tonic. Tonality comprises all twelve major and minor keys, as well as the scales, triads, and harmonic functions that define them.

tremolo   The rapid repetition of a single pitch or chord. Used for purposes of affective and dramatic intensification.

triplet   Three notes of equal value played in place of two notes of equal value.

Selected Bibliography

Avins, Styra, ed. *Johannes Brahms: Life and Letters*. Translations by Josef Eisinger and Styra Avins. New York: Oxford University Press, 1997.

Beller-McKenna, Daniel. *Brahms and the German Spirit*. Cambridge, Mass.: Harvard University Press, 2004.

Brown, Clive. *Classical and Romantic Performing Practice 1750–1900*. Oxford: Oxford University Press, 1999.

Couch, Leon W., III. "Voice Leading and Emotional Transformation in Brahms's Intermezzo in E-flat Minor, Op. 118, No. 6." Unpublished article, 2004.

Daverio, John. *Robert Schumann: Herald of a "New Poetic Age."* New York: Oxford University Press, 1997.

Frisch, Walter, ed. *Brahms and His World*. Princeton, N.J.: Princeton University Press, 1990.

The Harvard Dictionary of Music, 4th ed. Edited by Don Michael Randel. Cambridge, Mass.: Harvard University Press, 2003.

Hull, Kenneth. "Allusive Irony in Brahms's Fourth Symphony." In *Brahms Studies, Vol. 2*, ed. David Brodbeck. Lincoln: University of Nebraska Press, 1998.

Jankélévitch, Vladimir. *Music and the Ineffable*. Translated by Carolyn Abbate. Princeton, N.J.: Princeton University Press, 2003.

Kater, Michael H. *The Twisted Muse: Musicians and Their Music in the Third Reich*. New York: Oxford University Press, 1997.

Lang, Paul Henry. *Music in Western Civilization*. New York: Norton, 1997.

Le Van, Eric. "Brahms and the Fabric of Memory." Published as liner notes to *Brahms Sonatas No. 1 and No. 3*, Gallo CD-946.

————. Interview by Bernard Jacobson in *Fanfare*, January/February 2002.

Notley, Margaret. *Lateness and Brahms: Music and Culture in the Twilight of Viennese Liberalism*. New York: Oxford University Press, 2007.

The Oxford Companion to Music. Edited by Alison Latham. Oxford: Oxford University Press, 2002.

Painter, Karen. *Symphonic Aspirations: German Music and Politics, 1900–1945.* Cambridge, Mass.: Harvard University Press, 2007.

Ricci, Adam. "The Progress of a Motive in Brahms's Intermezzo Op. 119, No. 3." *Music Theory Online* 13, no. 3 (September 2007): http://mto.societymusictheory.org/issues/mto.07.13.3/mto.07.13.3.ricci.html.

Rosen, Charles. *Critical Entertainments: Music Old and New.* Cambridge, Mass.: Harvard University Press, 2000.

———. *The Romantic Generation.* Cambridge, Mass.: Harvard University Press, 1995.

———. *Romantic Poets, Critics, and Other Madmen.* Cambridge, Mass.: Harvard University Press, 1998.

Steinberg, Michael. *The Concerto: A Listener's Guide.* New York: Oxford University Press, 1998.

Swafford, Jan. *Johannes Brahms: A Biography.* New York: Alfred A. Knopf, 1997.

CD Track Listing

1. Symphony No. 3 in F major, Op. 90: First Movement—Allegro non troppo (10:34)
   Wilhelm Furtwängler, conductor, Berlin Philharmonic
   Ⓟ 2008 Music & Arts Programs of America, Inc. Courtesy of Music & Arts.
   From Music & Arts CD 4941

2. Sonata No. 3 in F minor, Op. 5: Second Movement—Andante (12:06)
   Eric Le Van, piano
   Ⓟ 2008 Gallo Records. Courtesy of Gallo Records.
   From Gallo Records CD 946

3. Sonata No. 3 in F minor, Op. 5: Fifth Movement—Finale (8:07)
   Eric Le Van, piano
   Ⓟ 2008 Gallo Records. Courtesy of Gallo Records.
   From Gallo Records CD 946

4. Ballade in B minor, Op. 10, No. 3 (4:01)
   Ian Lindsey, piano
   Ⓟ 2008 Ian Lindsey. Courtesy of Ian Lindsey.
   From private recording

5. Ballade in B major, Op. 10, No. 4 (8:43)
   Eric Le Van, piano
   Ⓟ 2008 Gallo Records. Courtesy of Gallo Records.
   From Gallo Records CD 1203

6. Rhapsody in G minor, Op. 79, No. 2 (6:39)
    Roberto Poli, piano
    ℗ 2008 Roberto Poli. Courtesy of Roberto Poli.
    From private recording

7. Intermezzo in B-flat minor, Op. 117, No. 2 (5:09)
    ℗ 2008 Roberto Poli. Courtesy of Roberto Poli.
    From private recording

8. Intermezzo in E minor, Op. 118, No. 6 (4:32)
    Jonathan Tsay, piano
    ℗ 2008 Jonathan Tsay. Courtesy of Jonathan Tsay.
    From private recording

9. Violin Concerto in D major, Op. 77: Second Movement—Adagio
    (9:21)
    Ginette Neveu, violin; Antal Dorati, conductor, The Hague Residentie
    Orchestra
    ℗ 2008 Music & Arts Programs of America, Inc. Courtesy of Music & Arts.
    From Music & Arts CD 837

10. *Ein Deutsches Requiem*, Op. 45: Fourth Movement—"Wie lieblich
    sind deine Wohnungen" (5:46)
    Wilhelm Furtwängler, conductor, Stockholm Konsertförenings Orkester/
    Musikalista Sällskapet Kör
    ℗ 2008 Music & Arts Programs of America, Inc. Courtesy of Music & Arts.
    From Music & Arts CD 1085

CD compilation © 2008 Amadeus Press

Like other authors in the Unlocking the Masters series, I have included on the accompanying CD recordings of internationally prominent and established concert artists. But I have also resolved to seek out and promote a number of extraordinarily gifted and imaginative concert artists who may not yet be household names, but whose virtuosity and exemplary musicianship distinguishes each of them as world class. To this end, I have incorporated recordings of performances by certain musicians made especially for this book, and below I have included some biographical information on the performers. In making this opportunity available to these artists, I look forward to introducing each of them to a wider audience, which I am confident will find their music making as rich, stimulating, and rewarding as I do.

Eric Le Van is an American-born pianist who has been praised by the critics and public alike for his original interpretations of the classical repertoire, particularly the music of Brahms and Scriabin. As a young artist, he remained an autodidact and a maverick. Interested in literature, history, and philosophy, he was also a violinist until turning full-time to the piano. At age twenty-one he moved to Europe, where he toured extensively and directed the Franz Liszt Festival in France for several years. He launched his recording career with a CD of Brahms's piano music, and critics soon hailed him as a major Brahms interpreter of exemplary depth and power. Le Van's subsequent releases of Liszt and Scriabin won unanimous praise, notably in the *American Record Guide, Gramophone, Neue Musikzeitung*, and *Le Monde de la Musique*. Le Van is also interested in making lesser-known composers and works available to the larger public through his recordings of Raff, Dussek, Toch, and Schoenberg, among others. He has been a guest soloist in major festivals and venues in the United States and Europe, including the Weimar Franz Liszt Festival and the International Beethoven Festival in Bonn, as well as the Kennedy Center and the Library of Congress in Washington, D.C. He currently lives in the United States. His website is www.ericlevan.com.

American pianist **Ian Lindsey** had captured the imagination of audiences and critics alike for the grand manner of the true Romantic style displayed in his playing, sporting a repertoire that encompasses the great cycles of Rachmaninoff's complete *Études-Tableaux* and Liszt's complete *Hungarian Rhapsodies*, which he has recently recorded. Mr. Lindsey is also at home in the works of Brahms, Beethoven, and Chopin. Graduating with honors from the New England Conservatory in Boston, he studied under the tutelage of renowned pianist Randall Hodgkinson. Lindsey has received numerous awards, and he now teaches a select group of talented pupils, in addition to giving acclaimed performances in the United States and abroad. More can be found online at www.garageband.com/artist/ian_lindsey.

Described as "a dancing musician with velvet muscles," Venetian-born pianist **Roberto Poli** has lived in the United States since 1998. He has studied with Giorgio Vianello (a pupil of Ferruccio Busoni's disciple Gino Tagliapietra) and Boris Petrushansky. He has studied at the New England Conservatory in Boston, where his teacher was legendary pianist Russell Sherman. Poli has earned a reputation as a rising authority on the music of Chopin, which he has comprehensively studied through manuscripts and original editions and has widely performed throughout the world, from his native Italy to Belgium, France, Ireland, Korea, Canada, Japan, and the United States. He is an active recording artist, and his debut recording *Shall We Dance . . .* was released in 2002 on the Americus Records label. For more information see www.roberto-poli.com.

Pianist **Jonathan Tsay** began his studies with Carolyn Savko at the age of five. Since then, he has pursued studies with Dr. Carol Leone at Southern Methodist University and with Marc Durand at l'Université de Montréal, where he will receive his doctorate in 2009. In addition to his critically acclaimed performances as a solo and chamber pianist, Jonathan is a regular presenter with the Van Cliburn Foundation's educational series Musical Awakenings. Most recently, Jonathan's series of multimedia lecture-recitals, "Between the Notes," aims to greater familiarize audiences with classical masterpieces through personal and anecdotal observations as well as historical and cultural context. Find out more at www.jonathantsay.com.